Success and Succession

Success and Succession

Unlocking Value, Power,
and Potential in the Professional
Services and Advisory Space

Eric Hehman, Jay Hummel,
and Tim Kochis

WILEY

Published by John Wiley & Sons, Inc., Hoboken, New Jersey.
Published simultaneously in Canada.

For general information on our other products and services or for technical support, please contact our Customer Care Department within the United States at (800) 762-2974, outside the United States at (317) 572-3993 or fax (317) 572-4002.

Wiley publishes in a variety of print and electronic formats and by print-on-demand. Some material included with standard print versions of this book may not be included in e-books or in print-on-demand. If this book refers to media such as a CD or DVD that is not included in the version you purchased, you may download this material at http://booksupport.wiley.com. For more information about Wiley products, visit www.wiley.com.

Library of Congress Cataloging-in-Publication Data:

Hehman, Eric, 1974-
   Success and succession : unlocking value, power, and potential in the professional services and advisory space / Eric Hehman, CFP, Jay W. Hummel, CFA, Tim Kochis.
      pages cm
   Includes bibliographical references and index.
   ISBN 978-1-119-05852-6 (cloth) ISBN 978-1-119-07148-8 (pdf)
ISBN 978-1-119-07135-8 (epub)
1. Executive succession. 2. Consulting firms–Management. 3. Business enterprises–Management. I. Hummel, Jay W., 1979- II. Kochis, Tim, 1946- III. Title.
   HD38.2.H44 2015
   001–dc23
                                                                    2015019101

Cover image: Old Rusty Locks ©iStock.com/JuhaHuiskonen
Cover design: Wiley

Printed in the United States of America

10 9 8 7 6 5 4 3 2 1

To those who will strive to be the next generations of leaders.

Contents

Section III: Emotional Challenges . . . and Solutions

Acknowledgments

Eric Hehman: To my wife, JayLeen, who has been the biggest blessing in my life and truly is my better half. Her confidence in me is unwavering and propelled me to take my initial job at Austin Asset as an unpaid intern. To my four young children: my hope is that someday, when they read this book, they will gain a deeper insight into their dad and know that even one person can make a difference in this world. To my parents, Curtis and Kathy, who modeled persistence and loyalty and inspired me to understand that slow and steady does win the race.

This story would not be possible without John Henry McDonald. His mentorship and partnership fueled my courage to be the leader I am today. To my partners at Austin Asset, Greg Van Wyk and Jonathan Davison, and our colleagues at Austin Asset, for joining me on this journey of building a business that we are all very proud of.

I am grateful to be surrounded by many wise mentors who challenge me to step beyond my limits: Larry Fehd, Tony Budet, Mark McClain, Jim Craver, Chris Hurta, Dave Helms, Rick Rhodes, Matt Burns, Trey Halbert, Matt Livingston, Jonathan Huffman, Mike Tipps, and Jeff Brown, when I needed your counsel, you were always there.

Bits and pieces of each of you are in this book. To the members of my study group, Xcelsior, for their incredibly helpful constructive feedback over the last 10 years.

The beauty of a project like this is learning from your coauthors and being affirmed by their shared insights. Tim has been a mentor from afar for many years. Whether he knew it or not, his sharing of his experience with a young kid from Texas was a real help to me. And to Jay, that infectious spirit of enthusiasm whom I met four years ago. Our minds raced to the adventures we might share one day. One day has come, my friend.

And, finally, I am deeply grateful to the clients I have learned from and served along the way. Your trust has been an enormous honor, and I hope that I can repay that gift by helping to build even a better way to exceed your expectations.

Jay Hummel: My wife and I like to call our family "Team Hummel." I could not have been blessed with better teammates than my wife, Valerie, and our two sons. Valerie's a rock star. She took care of a newborn and a two-year-old while I spent the weeks out of town doing my day job and most weekends at the neighborhood Starbucks trying to write. Her support never wavered, and if this book makes an impact, she's a big reason why.

I'm thankful for my friends Woody Taft, Jim Stengel, James Zimmerman, and Jim Bechtold, who inspired me to write this book when most people thought it was crazy. Thanks to Rob Densen, who challenged us on the original name of the book and graciously provided us with our final title. Chris Tankersley stepped up every time we asked him to help on draft formats even with unreasonable deadlines.

Tim agreed to write a book with two guys he barely knew. Thanks for taking a chance on us, Tim. We had a blast doing this together.

Last, thanks to my colleagues and friends at Envestnet, an amazing company with special people. Thanks to Jud, Bill, Jim, Zachary, and Lincoln, whose support of this effort has and will make a lasting difference.

Tim Kochis: Let me begin as close to the beginning as I can and thank my wife, Penelope Wong, not only for her patience and key advice throughout the effort to write this book but even more for her being at my side, every day, for the past 35 years of my professional career. I am also eager to acknowledge my colleagues at the old Kochis Fitz and the new Aspiriant for giving me the opportunity to experience these transitions of management and ownership, in very real terms, firsthand. With a few struggles here and there, the outcomes have been very good for me, and, I hope, even better for them.

Finally, I am eager to acknowledge Jay and Eric for the genuine pleasure of collaborating on this book. We weren't sure how a three-way responsibility for telling this story would play out, but we all quickly fell into comfortable patterns of contributing ideas, initiating drafts, negotiating differences, and editing to a final result, unified by a common purpose. We sincerely thank the many friends and industry colleagues for their wisdom and guidance in refining the views we present here. We owe them a huge debt for their gracious counsel, but take full responsibility for the miscues and inelegancies that may remain.

Most important, we thank and acknowledge the thousands of clients we have served and are serving, and the many more to come. Without them, there would be no reason to write this book. Fundamentally, this book is about them—and for them.

Introduction

This book grew out of an industry conference in 2013 in Dallas, Texas, hosted by financial industry journalist Bob Veres. Bob had asked Eric and Jay to come to Dallas to take part in a panel discussion, which he called the first of its kind, focused on successors talking to founders about the transition issues they faced in their businesses—from a successor's point of view. At the time, Jay was 33 and the president and chief operations officer (COO) of a large registered investment advisor and Eric was the 38-year-old chief executive officer (CEO) of Austin Asset.

There was a strong tone at the conference; the industry needed to hear more from successors. A day after Jay's and Eric's panel on transition issues for successors (also a day after Tim Kochis was given the conference's inaugural Leadership Award), Bob hosted a similar panel, but with members talking about their opinions as founders. The opinions from one day to another were similar in many respects, but there were clearly items where founders and successors materially disagreed. Instead of having two separate panels, it would have been an interesting social experiment to put the two points of view on one stage and thus try to do a better job of resolving the issues. We agreed that this book would become that stage.

The existing literature on succession tends to have a similar formula: What's been written was either written by a consultant, an academic, or a founder, usually after a successful transition. That formula will not apply in this book. Of course, the academic framework and successful stories have great relevance to the conversation. We have interviewed many industry observers and commentators and try to incorporate their wisdom in what follows. However, the truth is that more real-world experience is needed in this conversation. Transitions sometimes fail, not because of poor intentions, but because some unaddressed conflicts or other emotional or operational issues got in the way. Those who have actually been there can help others better navigate these often perilous waters.

A quick note on our backgrounds is relevant here. Tim is the ultimate founder. After an extremely successful run with his own firm, he and Rob Francais put their firms together and formed Aspiriant. Tim ran the firm as initial CEO for 22 months postmerger, and, as part of the merger plan, Rob then took on the leadership role to continue the firm's prominence as one of the largest and most highly respected independent wealth management firms in the country. Eric joined Austin Asset as an unpaid intern while attending the University of Texas. He joined the founder, and an early partner, as the third employee. His ascent to the CEO role of the firm is an up-and-down story, but has ended well for him and the firm's founder, with a successful transition. Jay is a senior vice president for one of the financial services industry's leading technology and consulting platforms, Envestnet Asset Management. His role at Envestnet, combined with his past experience as president and COO of a large RIA and his consulting background, makes him uniquely qualified to talk about the operational and succession issues firms face.

Transition issues are present regardless of which industry an advisory firm sits in and regardless of the firm's size. This book is not designed to be an academic exercise but, rather, a collaboration of industry thought leaders, practitioners, firms challenged by succession, firms not thinking about it, and firms that have made it to the other side of a successful transition. In our research and interviews, a common framework emerged.

For firms to successfully deal with succession and transition, they are required to do four things well:

1. Understand what the founders are trying to achieve and what the firm values and stands for.
2. Create a firm without founder dependency. The firm must come out on the other side with multiple capabilities built around a team.
3. Establish a governance and control model consistent with the needs of how the firm must operate to best serve clients.
4. Transition the equity of the firm in a way that is consistent with founder and successor desires.

These four common themes led to the structure of this book. The book is divided into the three sections we felt best embodied the difficulties of transitioning an advisory business: Operational Challenges, Financial Challenges, and Emotional Challenges. We deal with real or potential conflicts between founders and successors, bring in outside opinions from various industry leaders, and, we hope, deliver some important ideas to create a road map to success. Regardless of firm size, transition is tough. But size does matter, as we will explore. Sometimes it makes the transition easier; in other cases, it creates its own obstacles.

Founders and successors often have differing opinions, sometimes leading to conflict. We want to deal with this conflict openly and honestly to help firms successfully transition through these challenges.

This book is inspired by three central themes:

1. The transition process is about having choices and making them. Founders and successors will have dozens of choices to make during this process. Doing nothing is one such choice. And there are points throughout the transition where doing nothing is the right choice. However, those circumstances are rare. Doing something and choosing to be an active participant in the transition process leads to much higher levels of satisfaction for all involved.
2. Founders and successors are likely to sometimes disagree, sometimes very seriously. While this may be inevitable, it is not insurmountable. The advice in this book stems from the authors' experience-tested belief that an expectation of mutual respect should always start as the foundation and most often fosters the best outcomes.

3. Humility needs to drive the point of view from both sides. Founders could approach the transition process with the following point of view: "Heck with the successors and the employees. Don't they appreciate that without me they wouldn't even have their jobs? I built this firm and I will do whatever I want." Successors can have an equally emotional viewpoint: "Sure, the founder built the business, but now he's on the beach and I'm here putting in 60 hours a week to make the firm thrive. Without me here to take care of the place, the founder would sure be out of luck." Although we understand the legitimacy, in part, of both perspectives, not getting the transition process beyond this emotional level almost guarantees failure.

When we started this journey, we laid out the goals for this project: have fun working together; add, in a significant way, to the dialogue around one of our industry's most important business issues; and help founders and successors increase their odds of success in the process of transition. Thus far, we can assess completion on only one of these goals. We did have fun working through this effort. Whether we've achieved the other two are for you to judge. We hope we meet your needs. Enjoy the book.

Section I

OPERATIONAL CHALLENGES … AND SOLUTIONS

Chapter 1

The Founder as the Sun

All truths are easy to understand once they are discovered;
the point is to discover them.

—*Galileo Galilei*

The gravitational pull of the sun caused the formation of the planets
and set their orbits. Though planets are of different sizes and chemical
makeup, some orbit quickly, some slowly, and some even appear to move
backward. The system formed and remains in existence only because of
the sun.

A basic truth—the planets revolve around the sun—took many
thousands of years to become a commonly accepted perspective.
Geocentrism, which placed the Earth at the center of the universe, dom-
inated human thinking for thousands of years. We now know, of course,
that without the sun at the outset no planets would have formed, and
without the sun now the planets would drift into oblivion. Many advisory firms seem to operate in a similar manner: They arose and continue
to work because of the founder, and without the founder the company

would blow apart. But is what is true and necessary for our solar system the proper model?

The Evolution of a Founder-Centric Firm

It's easy to understand how founder-centric firms developed in the independent advisory space. They are the evolutionary result of the way in which many independent firms had to operate and grow to stay alive. The development trajectory of most independent firms is similar. In many cases, the founders graduated from college or advanced degree programs and landed at large corporations. In their younger years the work was exciting as they learned how to do what they wanted to do and how to sell themselves. Tim fits this profile: "When I was in my late 20s, I was at a large bank. It was exciting because we were part of a largely self-directed team, left to ourselves to figure it out as we went along. Here we were trying to provide financial advisory services to guys my dad's age. But it was exciting, in the early to mid-1970s, to be creating the advisory content and to learn to sell yourself. It was also fun. It was like a fraternity party, but we wore suits and ties."

Many founders fit a certain profile with the following traits: self-motivated, unafraid to ruffle feathers, open to risk, believing there's always a better way of doing things, and having an inner belief that investing in their own success will maximize their return. Look at that list again. Do these look like traits rewarded by most large companies?

As time goes on within many large corporations, entrepreneurial spirit gives way to centralizing control and managing overhead, especially within the reality of the economic cycle. When times get tough, corporations always protect their core businesses. If you aren't in the core channels, you aren't going to be able to command resources—or attention, as Tim lived through. This culture of central priorities and systematic decision making usually serves large corporations well, but tends to thwart new, small, or peripheral ventures. It drives many entrepreneurs to found their own shops.

Tim was frustrated by the obstacles his business was facing in a large accounting firm. Several significant clients asked why his small team wasn't just doing it on their own and even offered to invest behind them.

So, in 1991, Linda Fitz joined Tim in deciding it was time to invest in themselves and go independent as the original Kochis Fitz. The way in which advisory firms were founded is important to understand—and to celebrate—because those roots yield many of the strengths and the challenges the firms encounter in later transitions.

Also in 1991, David Cassady and Bob Schiller founded Cassady Schiller & Associates in Cincinnati, Ohio. In 23 years, the firm has grown from the two founding partners to 60 employees and now includes a wealth management practice. Both founders had spent 11 years at a Big Eight (now Big Four) accounting firm focused on small- and medium-size business and individual clients. They felt as though the model of the bigger firm was getting in the way of serving their clients. The triggering entrepreneurial moment for them was when a new regional partner came to the office and discussed the type of client the firm was going to focus on in the future. Bob explains how they felt that day: "This partner comes to Cincinnati and explains the firm is no longer after the clients paying us $20,000 a year because it wasn't big enough. We were stunned. How could this person not realize this profile represented 70 percent of the office's revenue and basically 100 percent of our practice? David and I realized we were no longer a fit."

The lack of the right home for their clients made it easy to decide to leave. As David puts it: "We knew we could do it better. We wanted to create a family culture in a business, which could stand the test of time, but worked really hard for the betterment of our clients' lives. We didn't start the firm because we wanted to run a business. We wanted the opposite … we wanted to spend more time with our clients." In the beginning, they couldn't afford office space, so they ran the firm out of their cars. At that time, cell phones were extremely expensive. They each had a $900 car phone bill the first month in business. David laughed when we sat down to interview him. Six weeks into the business, he wrecked his car: "We went from two office locations to one." Getting clients had to trump everything else because there were no clients. Each partner did eight sales meetings a day. After a month, they started winning a large amount of business. Things got easier from there.

David describes founding an advisory business as a little like the "wild, wild West." He continues, "When you start a firm, you are just trying to put the fires out. You aren't sitting at your desk thinking about best practices in operations." One example David describes was their pursuit of office space after a few months in business. They still didn't have any money, so they met with an owner of commercial and residential real estate to look at a few spaces. The guy realized they didn't have any money and suggested they barter for services, as he needed 14 federal Housing and Urban Development (HUD) audits completed. He asked David if the firm could complete the audits, and David said they could do them as a trade for leased office space. As they walked out of the meeting, Bob looked at David and said, "I didn't know you knew anything about HUD audits." "I don't," replied David. "But," he said, "we'll figure it out." They ended up having to hire a specialist, and it cost them more than just renting the office space would have. Bob describes it as a "valuable learning experience."

Throughout this book we highlight firms of all sizes, since most of the transition issues are similar regardless of firm size. The stories about David and Bob are great examples of a partner-founded firm that has grown from two partners to 60 employees. Jeff Thomasson is an example of a founder who has built a mega firm. Oxford Financial, founded in 1981, has grown to be one of the largest independent financial advisory firms in the country. When Jeff started the firm, he had just become one of the youngest graduates of the Indiana University MBA program, at the age of 22. His thesis for graduation was written on the topic of what a great financial firm should look like in the future. He walked off campus already feeling like a seasoned entrepreneur. Part of how he paid his way through college was buying Farrah Fawcett posters in bulk for $2 and selling them to his dorm mates for $5. After graduation, he grabbed a phonebook and started calling banks and business owners.

Jeff believed that if he cold-called as hard as he could for three years, he would never have to do it again. As he reflects on this goal, he feels lucky: "I only had to do it for two years!" Jeff realized he was great at getting an appointment, and he won some early business owners. Banks took notice of his different approach to financial planning, and they didn't see him as a threat. "I was a little guy. I wasn't going to take their trust business, so they sent me referrals." Like David and Bob, Jeff's office was his car. His monthly cell phone bill was $1,000. His stories of the founding also show how different things are today from 1981. "In 1981, cell phones were so rare in Midwest America you looked pretentious if you had one. You also had a large antenna on your car, so you couldn't hide the fact that you had one. I didn't want the banks to get the wrong idea. I would park down the street and walk to my appointments."

When most independent advisory firms were founded, advice was delivered not through technology, but through the human interaction of the founders and clients. The founder had his or her name on the door. In many instances, very early on, there wasn't the financial ability to hire much help The advice was delivered directly by the founder to the client. There was no need for process and no need for consistency in delivering the service or advice. The founder had to do everything.

Bill Crager, president of Envestnet, tells a funny story about how it feels to go from a big company to running and building your own start-up. He and others decided to leave the comfort of Nuveen to create a new business model in financial services. They finally got office space, and Bill took the lead in ordering the furniture for the office. "I was really happy to have it coming to the office so I could put my computer on something. Having furniture was a major step for our start-up." Bill's excitement turned to laughter when the furniture arrived unassembled. "I remember looking at two interns we had hired and saying, 'Well, I guess we need to find a hammer.' Have you ever tried to find a hammer to buy in downtown New York City?" Bill traipsed around New York and finally found a hammer. He got back to the office and then realized, "Why didn't I buy three? We shared the tool and eventually got it all put together. It's a memory I look back on fondly but not something I want to do again! This 'nobody else is going to do it so I have to' attitude becomes a habit … and, with success, often becomes a source of pride. Many successors simply wouldn't understand."

We examine many different sizes and types of firms and a wide variety of people throughout this book. Although these firms have made different choices as they evolved and are now in many different situations, the founders share consistent experiences and tell similar stories about their early years. These are amazing stories of entrepreneurship, risk, and success. This shared experience even creates a comradery around founding a firm. We call it the "fraternity of founders." Successors can learn from and celebrate this fraternity, but they will never be members. Successors don't have these types of stories. This lack of a common history and set of experiences can cause significant operational and emotional issues during leadership transitions. It is extremely important for successors and founders to recognize this crucial fact.

Is My Firm Founder-Centric?

One might assume a firm would know whether it was a founder-centered firm. However, many founders and successors are too busy to notice. Or maybe they don't really care.

If you want to determine whether a firm is founder-centric, the first place to look is often the founder's family. They will know the answer.

To confirm or determine whether a firm is founder-centric, we suggest a founder ask him or herself the following four questions:

1. When was the last time I took a week of uninterrupted vacation?
2. Have other members of the staff ever run client meetings?
3. When a bad event happens in a client's life, does the client only call the founder?
4. Do employees have the opportunity to make company decisions, or does everything go through the founder, even, for example, how the company handles a holiday party?

You get the idea; most people can stop at the first question.

Awareness

A successful transition process requires a keen sense of awareness on the part of both the founder and the successor. We studied extensively the way successors and founders can increase their ability to gain insights.

Gary Klein, in his 2013 book, *Seeing What Others Don't: The Remarkable Ways We Gain Insights,* lays out the foundational differences between gaining insight and missing it:

Flawed Beliefs: We can all fall prey to basing our decisions on flawed beliefs. The flawed belief that consumers wanted a new taste in soft drinks led to the disastrous rollout of New Coke in 1985. MySpace's flawed belief that it had created a superior technology platform and a high barrier for competitive entry led to the dismissal of Facebook as a worthy competitor. Facebook, in March of 2015, sits with a $232 billion market cap, and few people now even remember MySpace. Decca Records' flawed belief that four-piece bands were no longer the future of music led to their refusal to sign the Beatles, the most famous band of all time. Of course, nobody intentionally bases their decisions on beliefs they know to be flawed. Hindsight is always 20/20. The only way to overcome flawed beliefs is to shed light on their shortcomings. We use our research and experience to shed light on some flaws in founder and successor thinking throughout this book. There are three fundamentally flawed beliefs associated with founder-centric firms, which an industry leader described simply as "absolutely wrong."

The first flawed belief of founder-centric firms is "Nobody can run my firm the way I ran it." While, of course, nobody is going to run a firm exactly like the founder, successful firms don't need to be run exactly the same way. There are plenty of successors with more than enough ability to replace founders in the transition of firm management. Their accumulated insights and fresh perspective may make them even better at the task. Philip Palaveev is CEO of the Ensemble Practice LLC, a business management consulting firm focused on the evolution of team-based advisory businesses. He uses this analogy: "Founders not expecting changes to their businesses is a lot like selling your house and expecting the new owners not to remodel it."

The second flawed belief is "The young people can't afford to buy me out or don't want to take the risk to buy me out." If the founder can sell the vision and be reasonable, successors will buy.

The third flawed belief of founder-centric firms is "My firm is worth five times revenue because that's what I saw in the latest trade magazine." There's no one-size-fits-all methodology to determining firm value, but this raw comparative methodology often ends up with a delusional valuation, making it next to impossible to transition ownership of the firm.

Lack of Experience: Dr. Klein's research studied 120 cases of material insights, where one individual missed a situation while the other nailed it. Two-thirds of the insights in those cases depended on experience.

Many firms remain founder-centric because of inexperience, on both sides, in going through the transition process. This is almost certainly the most important business decision a founder ever makes. Getting it wrong can be catastrophic. And it's hard to do a trial run. The same inexperience in the face of critically important decision making is true for a successor as well. But, at least, first-round successors can learn from this to better facilitate their own transition of ownership and management to their successors. In any event, the stakes are very high and the experience levels are very low. That pressure leads many firms to do nothing.

A Passive Attitude: For many founders, transition is on their "important" list, but it's not urgent. In doing research for this book, we talked to founders who asked why they should care. "Why isn't the status quo okay?" It will take us the entire book to thoroughly answer that question, but here are some of the counterinquiries: Do you care if your clients will continue to be well-served through the indefinite future? Do you care if your firm has true equity value—for yourself and for others? Do you care about your durable legacy?

These questions are nearly impossible to answer if founders have a passive attitude about the transition process. So we urge founders to take an active stance, to start thinking seriously about what this journey will entail, and to actively address truths about founder-centric firms.

Management as Distinct from Ownership: This is one of the most fundamental insights that successful transitions deploy. Ownership is about value, dividends, and ultimate control. Management is about responsibility, performance, accountability, and compensation. The two dimensions are always united in founders; they can be separated in successors—at different times, in different measures, and through different persons. As Tim puts it: "Management is a job, ownership is a status; when the two combine, well, it's a happy coincidence, but the combination is not necessary".

No Successor: Good successors are patient and respectful of the founders of firms, but they won't sit still indefinitely. Founder-centric firms lack the organizational foundation for growth and provide little opportunity for successors (of several future generations) to develop talent and build personal wealth.

Paralyzed by Indecision: Many founders are stuck in a tough position: They don't really want to work as hard in the business as they used to, but they aren't going to move on from what they currently have until they decide what they want to do next. The emotional journey of running away from something versus running toward something can take its toll on both the founder and the successor. Founders may not want to keep the firm founder-centric, but they feel paralyzed with indecision.

Driven by Greed: Founders and successors trying to maximize every last penny from the past or future valuation of the business will not be successful in transition. Firms whose people harbor unreasonable valuation expectations—either much too high or much too low—will not transition.

No Legacy: The legacy of a founder-centric firm is limited to the charitable goodwill of the founder. A founder-centric firm can be financially generous, but the legacy stops there. The lack of transition leaves the clients and employees wanting but not getting more.

No Glass Elevator: In the final scene of the movie *Willy Wonka and the Chocolate Factory*, as a reward for his honesty, Charlie is granted a ride in a magical elevator. This magical elevator goes up the shaft and breaks through the ceiling, flying Charlie around the sky and giving him a different perspective. He's no longer constrained by the physical structure. Founder-centric firms have no glass elevator, as they are constrained by their business models. Founder-centric firms have limited leverage, driven by their capacity constraints. These constraints come as the founder either maxes out capacity or decides he or she wants to focus more on his or her own life than on the business. This lack of capacity leads to decaying growth.

Missing What Drives Value: Mark Tibergien, CEO of Pershing Advisor Solutions, discussed with us a very simple concept founder-centric firms fail to understand. "Valuation is a function of the future." The lack of a sustainable growth model in a founder-centric firm diminishes the equity value of a firm … perhaps to zero. It's easy to see how founder-centric firms, focused just on today, can miss this reality. Without future sustainability, without ongoing satisfied clients and solid continuing revenue, the firm could end up worthless.

Waiting Too Long: In theory, it's never too late to start a transition because a firm can always find a buyer for the right price—the buyer's right price. That price may not equal the amount of effort and work put into building a firm.

Reasoning Style: Whether someone has a concrete or open reasoning style is usually a personality trait. This is not to say a person with a concrete, black-and-white reasoning style can't gain insights; it's just more likely that new insights are going to come from a style that is open to tangents rather than a fixed destination.

As successors, Jay and Eric struggle with this one the most. As Eric explains, "Often, the successor is more a businessperson, bringing structure to the business to complement a charismatic, intuitive founder. The successor often needs to be concrete in decisions and to bring consistency and predictability to the company. This points to the opportunity to advance the process around their different strengths." Often, founders have the advantage here. You may just need to spur them to their own creative aptitudes and their taste for vision. What would make a truly inspiring future?

"The Painters"

Successful transitions are an evolution not a revolution. Philip Palaveev spends most of his time helping advisory firms create better organizations. Philip describes a story from a forum he moderated; it serves as an inspiration for enhanced awareness in transition efforts. At a session focused on success with both founders and successors present, one founder stood up and eloquently described how creating a business seemed to him a lot like painting a picture. He wanted the picture to be beautiful and to be preserved so that many could see and appreciate it. A successor quickly jumped up and explained the problem with this view. The successor said "You are missing the point. We are artists, too; we want to keep on painting the picture."

Many firms became a masterpiece because founders were visionary enough at the outset to see there was a better way of doing things for their clients and lots of room for improvement in their business models. They were the founders starting fee-based firms in the financial advisory space. They were founders paving the way for a new business model around financial planning, designing financial plans on dot matrix printers, or even on yellow legal pads, and using handheld calculators.

They were accountants realizing there was a model built not only on compliance and tax returns but on becoming business advisors and developing deeper relationships with their clients. These founders rose to the occasion in the face of great challenges and created new opportunity for their clients—and, in so doing, for themselves.

Successors can achieve the same kinds of accomplishments if they are given the chance. In all industries that advisory businesses serve, there are great challenges ahead. The world is becoming more complex for the clients they serve. Advisory services firms cannot expect to be immune. Technology is advancing, regulatory costs are rising, and expectations for the services provided are rising while prices are falling. There is no lack of ongoing challenge, and there's no lack of opportunity for ongoing entrepreneurial success by the successors to the initial pioneers. As Bernie Clark, executive vice president at Charles Schwab, puts it: "Regulation is going to impose [a] much greater burden on advisory firms, probably fostering more combinations, but forcing much more sophisticated firms in any event."

So founders cannot expect successors to treat their firms like masterpieces in a museum. Successful firms don't hang on walls and remain unchanged. Herein lies the lesson. The remainder of this book is about conflict. It's about a celebration of the masterpiece founders have created, but it's also about the difficult necessity of change. This book is about making founders and successors realize they have something in common: Both of them are painters. They want the best for their firms and clients. The transition process requires founders and successors to grab a new canvas. Let's paint.

KEY TAKEAWAYS:

1. It's perfectly normal for a firm to be founder-centric. Many successful firms grew up this way because of the operational realities of building a successful advisory business. No apologies are necessary.
2. A firm needs to be honest with itself about whether or not it is founder-centric and understand the challenges this may or may

not present for the future. If a firm genuinely wants to transition, it cannot remain founder-centric.

3. There are fundamentally flawed beliefs that exist in many founders' minds and in the advisory business industry. If not overcome, those flawed beliefs will likely doom the transition process.

4. The transition process has to celebrate the achievements of the founder and the firm. Both founders and successors have to be "running to something," not "running away from something."

5. Founders and successors should revisit the awareness discussion. For a firm to transition effectively, it requires both founders and successors to gain effective insights at the proper times.

Chapter 2

Replacing the Sun:
A New Solar System

The conductor of an orchestra doesn't make a sound. He depends, for his power, on his ability to make other people powerful.

—*Benjamin Zander*

Remember when you passed your driver's test and received your license? It was an indescribable feeling of joy, freedom, fear, and excitement all rolled into one. This is the feeling many successors have as they take over a firm from a founder or group of founders. Removing the founder from the day-to-day operations of the firm has an emotional impact on everyone involved: the founder, successor, employees, community partners, and, of course, the clients. We deal with the emotional aspects of this transition later in the book, but in this chapter we focus on the operational risks successors and founders need to evaluate in their transition.

The founder-centric firm, so common in the advisory space, creates a challenge for the successor in assessing the organization and what it needs to grow. The successor and founder should start with one question: Are we replacing the old model with a new model or are we just placing a new person at the center of the solar system? The answer to this question has major ramifications throughout the organization, and for its employees and clients.

What Road Do You Choose?

Two roads diverged in a wood, and I—
I took the one less traveled by,
And that has made all the difference.

—*Robert Frost*

This idea of choice continues to guide our thinking. Since the three of us are "glass half full" people, we read this ending and believe the "difference" made is a positive one. Most people likely read the poem and interpret it in a positive way. However, cynics will say there's no clear answer. Maybe the other road is less traveled for good reason; there may be great dangers ahead. Founders are often not only choosing a road but clearing the land to lay the beginnings of a road—a safe passage to a destination not yet seen. By the time the successor comes along, he or she is in a position to level the road, perform maintenance, and often lay pavement to expand the capacity it can handle.

Firms choosing to remain independent and build a second and then further generations of leaders, have two roads in front of them. We believe that the "road highly traveled" leads down a path where the founder is simply substituted at the center of the firm's solar system. The founder copies his or her role description and just hands it to the successor. The processes of the firm and the skill sets of the people are not reassessed, and changes (improvements) to the client experience are not at the center of the transition. Many firms believe this is a viable approach, and for some firms it is. It has the benefit of being least disruptive in the short term. It maintains continuity around people and the business model. However, in our opinion, this short-term continuity can create significant longer-term challenges. It's the "if it ain't broke, don't fix it strategy." As in the story of the little Dutch boy, Hans Brinker, who put his finger in the dike to stop a leak, this is not likely to be a permanent solution. Tomorrow's problems are always lurking behind the distractions of today's busy schedule. We believe short-term thinking in the operational components of transition can lead to longer-term challenges for both successors and founders. These longer-term challenges impact the ability to monetize the business, enhance the client experience, and successfully transition the firm to future leadership.

The "road less traveled," where the client experience, staffing decisions, and new growth opportunities are addressed, is hard. It's especially so on the successor as the one being tasked first with maintaining and then growing and improving the business. In many cases the founder has already reduced his or her workload and it's easy for a successor to get trapped in a rut of just trying to get daily tasks accomplished. Successors may believe they are heading down the road less traveled, but if they don't follow a deliberate operational approach to the transition, they can easily be detoured to the first, highly traveled road, without even noticing. We believe the hard work of choosing the more onerous short-term path leads to a company with better prospects for growth, with a culture that can recruit and retain top talent, and one that is better poised to achieve good outcomes for clients, employees, and the firm's owners as well.

Committing to the Road Less Traveled

If the founder and the successor have chosen to take the longer-term view, what's next?

As a successor, you may already be an owner in the firm or are about to become an owner and operator of the firm. Now what do you do? The first step is to evaluate the involvement of the founder. Is the founder going to be involved in the day-to-day management and operation of the business? Is the founder going to transition to a new role immediately, or over some period of time? The speed at which you must assess the client experience, organizational processes, and staff resources will differ based on the transition period. If the founder remains involved, don't worry too much. Take your time and get it right, but be very clear about where the ultimate authority lies. And be sure that the founder has an adequately engaging area of responsibility so he or she doesn't

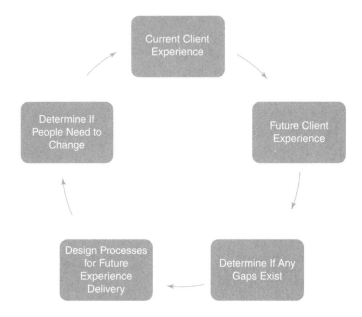

Figure 2.1 The Operational Assessment Process

even inadvertently try to reoccupy his or her former space. If, instead, your founder truly retires, turn on an old Road Runner cartoon and take some notes; you have no choice but to dig right in.

Figure 2.1 provides a framework in which to evaluate the operational needs of the business.

Assessing the Client Experience

The Founder or the Firm?

The successor needs to assess the operational significance of the founder. To do this, start with one dominant perspective: not your own, not the founder's, but the client's perspective. How does the client view the firm? How do the processes work to serve the client? Are there repeatable, documented processes in place, or did everything rely on the patterns, opinions, talents, and relationships of the founder?

We believe there are a number of steps a firm should go through to assess the client experience. This process is laid out in Figure 2.2.

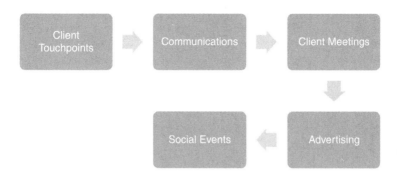

Figure 2.2   Assessing the Client Experience

The Supplemental Materials to this book include a form that helps to catalog all of the firm's client touchpoints. The key through this entire assessment is to ask four main questions: Who? When? Why? How?

The client communication assessment step tells a firm a lot about where it is in transition. We believe a successor needs to review all the touchpoints with a client. Who schedules meetings? How are they scheduled? When newsletters and other communications go out, under what name are they released? Whether you have a founder-centric firm or a client-centric firm will become obvious. If all communications have come out under the founder's cover, you haven't transitioned the firm in the eyes of the client. You can always tell the stage of transition the firm is in and how hard it could be on the successor by looking at the last five general client communications.

Eric agrees that communications are an appropriate start, and he cautions: "This operational assessment is tough work, but it's important. You need to realize no detail is too small. We had a very detailed process which started with something as small as a newspaper advertisement." John Henry McDonald was the founder and the face of Austin Asset. He brought in almost all of the clients. He was on the radio and was the voice of the company. To make the point that this might need to change, Eric began to talk with John Henry about the firm's advertisements. Since its founding, Austin Asset had run advertisements with a picture of John Henry and his dog. People saw the ads, maybe recognized his name from the radio, and would call the company. This is where Eric started to worry. As John Henry began transitioning away from the business, what was the receptionist going to tell the prospect? John Henry isn't here? John Henry will call you back? Let me put you through to someone else? It was not a small detail. It could become a big issue in the day-to-day operations of the business.

Over time, the firm transitioned its marketing. The first step was to retain the picture of John Henry and his dog but add the other members of the firm. The final step added the logo and a picture of all the advisors, but did not include the names of any individual advisors in the ad. This took time because it carried an emotional weight, but Austin Asset needed to show prospects that the entire firm, and not just the founder, had something to offer. Similarly, market outlooks and newsletters, quotes in the newspaper, articles written in trade publications, and conference speeches all have important impacts on the business's ongoing success through a transition. The founder has the ability to endorse others in the firm and elevate their visibility.

Eric shares this story: At his first industry conference with John Henry, he was invited onstage during the preparation the night before the presentation. He had been with the firm for a couple of years, but had never been put in a position like this with the founder and another industry veteran (David Drucker). Much to his surprise, the next day he was included in the actual live presentation on career paths and from that day forward was encouraged to share his story with other young practitioners. This endorsement also helped back home at the firm. He was starting to develop his own voice, under the guidance of his mentor/founder.

Tim's case was different. He had always been the "voice" of the firm, authoring or editing virtually every word that Aspiriant or Kochis Fitz had published and being the primary spokesperson to media and the industry. He continued in that role to design the firm's transition communications, but then choreographed his own obsolescence as the firm's voice, promoting a greater public presence for Rob Francais and replacing his editorial role with a fresh editorial committee.

It's Show Time—The Meeting Strategy

In the advisory space, most of the client experience comes down to the in-person meeting with clients. Founders of successful advisory firms love client meetings—they're like a show. A lot of work goes on behind the scenes that clients don't fully appreciate because they don't see it. This puts a lot of pressure on the advisors and support staff to represent the firm's brand when they are onstage. As most successful founders of advisory businesses are really very good at selling and love being onstage, looking at the client meetings and how they will work during and after the transition is one of the most important operational decisions a company makes.

The Agenda: All successful meetings have an agenda, but in the transition process who sets the agenda for client meetings? The answer is simple in some firms, but complicated in others. Both Eric and Jay set the agenda in their respective firms. Both believed it was a good step in the learning process, especially when taking on new responsibility for the relationships, to review past meeting notes to see if they could zero in on what the client really was interested in. Jay believes taking an extra step helps to encourage a growing relationship with clients. "I believe in all cases, but especially when you are trying to build a new relationship, you should call a client or prospect two weeks before the meeting, give them some preliminary thoughts you have on the agenda, and ask them what they want included. It goes a long way to show you are prepared, are empathetic, and are genuinely interested in meeting the client's needs. It certainly gives you a better chance of having a good meeting."

Train Wrecks to Avoid

The next step is to determine whether the founder needs to review the agenda with the successor in advance. We strongly encourage this during the transition process. The founder and successor should not only understand the subject items but also assign who is going to speak on which topics. In some cases, the founder may no longer be attending every meeting with a client. Sometimes a founder doesn't want to take the time to review the agenda or the materials. The successor or someone else in the firm is now the day-to-day relationship manager and understands the issues and the client's goals for the meeting.

The successor relationship manager and the founder enter the meeting room. Two things can go awry. The first train wreck involves the founder bringing up a "hot topic" that had already been resolved at a previous meeting, making the founder, and the firm, look out of touch. How do you think that makes a client feel? The person they have trusted for many years to look after them suddenly appears to be out of the loop.

According to Tim, this potential problem is completely controllable. As the firm grows, primary client service responsibility transitions need to take place, client by client, long before the founder steps away from the overall leadership of the firm. You need to make sure the client understands there is someone looking after the details. Tim explains: "This may no longer be my responsibility as much as it was before, but I need to be transparent and honest with the client. I can't have it both ways. I either have control of the relationship and therefore must be all over it, or I need to tell the client I am there to support and mentor the successor client relationship manager. Often, perhaps, I'm not going to know all of the details, but the successor will." At first, this can require a leap of faith in the skills of the new manager of the client relationship; for a founder, it takes humility.

Another potential train wreck can have more long-term ramifications for the firm. We'll describe this problem as "does not play well with others." It can be hard for the founder to refrain from stepping back in where he or she left off and dominating an entire meeting. Eric describes how it feels when a successor watches this in real time: "Founders have built very successful businesses, in many cases with them virtually doing everything. They are wired to continue that; and they step into the meeting and dominate it. As I would watch it happen I would think to myself, this doesn't do any good for our transition. Successors have to be prepared and work hard to command the agenda items most important to the client. It's easy in the beginning to feel apprehensive. You may not present things same way as founder or present them as well. You and the founder, both, have to learn to be okay with this reality."

At Austin Asset, Eric and John Henry went through role-playing exercises. That role-play didn't start with the meeting; it started the moment the client walked in the door. Eric walks us through his thought process: "I was worried about the little details of relationship building. Should I greet the client? Should John Henry? Should the receptionist just sit them in the room? We worked really hard to transition relationships and to have clients feel comfortable about John Henry not being their day-to-day relationship manager. If a client spent the first

10 minutes catching up with John Henry on the weather and other small talk, that's one thing. In a supportive role to the team, he could do what he did best: relate to anyone and make them feel welcome. However, sometimes clients would talk hard details and then John Henry would find himself knee-deep into a planning topic without really wanting to disrupt the process. For founders it is through no real fault of their own or bad intention. These skills are what attracted the client to them in the first place. But this overexerted strength of their own can become a weakness for the business transition. It takes a brave successor and a self-aware founder to replace this client reliance."

Other details that both Jay and Eric analyzed were: Who was in the meeting and how should the room be configured? Both of them believed the person heading the meeting should be at the table or located in the room in a way that made it obvious to the client that this person was in charge of the meeting. Founders and successors need to have a plan before the meeting. Let's get very practical and lay out what we think is an effective way to handle this subtle interaction.

For instance, if the founder greets the client and has a pleasant two- or three-minute interaction *and* then endorses the "new" client lead before walking into the meeting, the stage is set for a positive transition of client responsibility. The founder escorts the client to the meeting room, where the "new" lead is positioned at the head of the table, with the founder maybe at the side of the "new" lead. The "new" lead welcomes the client and builds rapport before taking the lead in conducting the meeting with a clear agenda. The founder's role is to support the advice of the lead and, as the meeting closes, might offer a comment like this: "Joe will be following up with your next steps and action items. I will be only a phone call away, but look to Joe first for any follow-up questions you have." Then the follow-up e-mail traffic begins, and the founder is copied on all of it. As the next meeting approaches, the successor can take the next step. At that next meeting, the "new" client service lead can greet the client at the outset, with the founder's speaking role restricted to the meeting itself, planned only to add color or perspective and perhaps close the meeting with an empathetic question. One of John Henry's great closing comments was: "Are we doing what you would have us do for you?" It demonstrated concern that he genuinely cared that the client was being well served through the transition to a new advisor.

Taking the Long View

The decision at Austin Asset not to put John Henry and his dog in the newspaper was a risky proposition in the short term. Eric worried. What if the phone quit ringing? This is where very real conversations can occur, and should occur, about expectations. "In our case I was a minority owner and the reality was that John Henry made the call to pull the picture from the ad. We certainly talked a lot about 'why' this was important for him, for me, for the firm and for clients we didn't even have yet. The tide changed and we found the phone rang more than it ever did before." The beauty was that now John Henry didn't have to work with every person who called. John Henry could close business like Mariano Rivera, Major League Baseball's all-time leader in saves. Tim Kochis could as well. Most successful founders can close at high rates. If they couldn't, they wouldn't have a business to transition. But to have the founder continuing to close all the business means that others aren't learning how to do it—they are being given the fish rather than learning how to fish for themselves.

Good businesses grow. As Section II of this book examines, a firm's growth rate is one of the most important variables driving at its equity value. The long-term track record of the firm matters more than a short-term decline or a positive spike. This economic reality is easy to understand academically, but for a firm in transition it can be difficult to deal with the idea of a short-term pullback in growth. As the successors and their team take on the responsibility of generating new business, a firm hopes the growth rate will increase and stabilize. The growth rate in the first year of a transition often drops. This is driven by two key factors. As a founder-centric firm shifts its brand, fewer prospects may come in the door, and the close rate of the successor may not be as high as the founder's was. Further, the operational work we discuss in this chapter is important to rebuild the foundation for the firm's future. That can be extremely time consuming, leaving less time and energy, in the short term, for business development efforts.

Austin Asset conducted a very relevant conversation during its time of transition. With the desire of the growth-minded founder focused on business development and the successor intent on building a system that could sustain itself, John Henry and Eric had to get on the same page. The "help" of more new client activity was actually "hurting" the business. Eric went to John Henry and said what must have sounded blasphemous to say to a natural rainmaker: "The best thing you can do right now is *not* bring in any new clients." Why? Because the firm was in the middle of an entire service model revision centered on three pillars of progress—a new client experience, an ongoing retention experience, and a new staff compensation model.

1. **New client experience:** How would we screen potential clients? How would we schedule those that were a fit? How would we manage the meeting? What roles would the team play? What would the founder's role be?
2. **Ongoing retention:** How often would we meet? What would we offer at those meetings? How would we prepare for those meetings? What roles would the team play in those meetings (if different from those listed in "New Client Experience")? How would we handle quarterly reports or other communications with clients?
3. **Compensation:** Does it matter which clients you specifically work with? Would it be team oriented or production based? How would we reward a collaborative model where clients belong to the firm? How would we structure a model with a competitive base and team-focused incentives, aligned to the organization's overall strategy?

It really does little good for a founder and successor to bring a high volume of prospects in the door if new processes are not yet in place to match or, better, improve the client experience. According to a 2014 Schwab benchmarking study, 75 percent of all new business in financial advisor firms comes to the high-performing firms through referrals. So bringing a prospect in the door for a bad experience can really hurt the brand of the firm. For a while during the transition, a firm needs to be more internally focused. Short-term pullbacks in growth are okay. Nevertheless, founders and successors need to have a discussion about how long they are willing to accept that slowdown. If you allow the transition to drag on, it's easy to lose focus on external relationships and all the other things needed to build a growth-oriented culture. Firms that stay internally focused too long don't grow.

Welcome to McDonald's: May I Take Your Order?

One of the University of Notre Dame's legendary Knute Rockne's most famous lines was "I find prayers work better when I have bigger players." Our advisory businesses are built on our advice. Advice is delivered by people. If logic holds, then better people and better advice produce a better-performing firm. As a successor, there is nothing more important than making the right people decisions. This is obvious on paper but difficult in practice. Charles Goldman, one of the financial industry's most experienced observers and most insightful thinkers, sums it up: "Building the best business you can ... the best people ... the best processes ... will make your transition much easier. Through the transition process people often lose sight that in the end it's about building a better business."

One of the hardest things successors have to do is assess the people they inherit. Depending on how long the successor is in place at the firm, he or she may have been involved in hiring most of the people. Most successors inherit at least an employee or two as the "legacy" hires of the founders. A common theme throughout this book is the respect due to founders for taking the risk to go on their own and create a business, often largely from nothing. It takes a special kind of person to do this. It also takes a healthy ego and strong self-confidence. This confidence leads to success in building the business, but it can cause problems in many areas during the transition. The people element is one area where problems often lurk.

Despite good intentions, founders' egos sometimes get in the way of making optimal people decisions. We've seen two types of founders. The first type hires people smarter than themselves and lets those people excel. The reason many transitions don't work is that too many founders are in the second category. They love being the center of attention and insist on being the smartest person in the room. This pride in being the best causes them to surround themselves with lower-performing employees, rewarding loyalty and deference instead of high performance. These firms tend to have hired "order takers" rather than self-initiators. They sit at their desk and wait to be told what to do. Which kind of founder the firm has had should give you a good sense of the kind of people you have inherited.

Human Capital Framework

The Supplemental Materials provides a framework that is focused on the people involved in the firm. This supports a systematic process for the firm to go through to make logical decisions about their people. People decisions are hard. A key finding from the 2014 Schwab benchmarking study is that the fastest-growing firms believe that what brought them to their current level of success is not enough to take them to the next. This almost certainly includes at least some of your people.

Question #1: Would you hire this person again, knowing what you know today?

Jay reflects on this question: "I've made some bad hires. I think we all have at some point in our career. I went back over the bad hires I've made and they all raised the same thought: I wish I could go back and not hire that person. I realized when assessing existing organizations: Why not force yourself to ask this question to bring clarity? If you wouldn't hire someone again if given the chance, should they really be on your team?"

Question #2: Is the person meeting the expectations for their role today, and whether they are or not, can they learn and grow into rising expectations?

Every high-performing organization should have expectations for each role. If people aren't meeting the minimum expectations today, should they be around? The response to that question from an operational viewpoint is simple. How about three years from now? We live in a service economy. The client experience is the focus of every service organization. Clients know this and continually increase their expectation of what a good client experience looks like. Advisory businesses are no exception. The expectations of service delivery increase; consequently, the performance expectations for your people need to increase with it.

Having a culture that fosters raising the level of performance is important and can be accomplished only if that is a part of your performance appraisal process. The performance appraisal process does not need to be complex. Larger organizations often have a formal human resources program to manage this. Smaller firms may merely meet casually with employees once a year over lunch. Whatever works for your firm is fine so long as a "better than average" performance today becomes only "average" performance three years from now, and average performance today may be considered an unsatisfactory level at some time in the future. One way to begin to get this across is to have employees list their top 10 accomplishments each year as part of a self-appraisal process. This allows you to see how employees view their roles, what's important to them, and what they are proud of. If you do this each year you can compare the accomplishments, year over year, to see if their positive impact on the business has increased.

Question #3: Is this person the best person I can hire for the job?

No matter the size of your firm, best-in-class organizations have best-in-class people. This question is more subjective than the other questions in the framework. What does "best in class" mean? Like beauty, it's in the eye of the beholder, but here are some simple situations to consider. Do you ever rave about your employees at an industry event or cocktail party? When you go to conferences and hear the speaker, do you ever think that your people are as good as or better on the substantive topic or in their presentation skills? If so, you probably do have the best in class.

However, this exercise raises a further question: Do all of my people need to be best in class? Best-in-class talent is expensive. Why should I pay top dollar to have best-in-class people in every position? The next filter helps assign weights to the first three questions in the framework.

Question #4: Is the position critical?

We believe a company should have a culture where all roles are rewarded and equal amounts of appreciation are given for jobs well done. However, leaders all know certain roles are more important than others. A receptionist is further down the food chain than your lead business development position. We recommend that successors rank each position in order of importance: critical, important, or replaceable. This can help bring clarity to the first three questions. If you mark a position as important or replaceable but not critical, you likely don't need someone who is best in class in that position. You may be able to deal with someone who just meets general expectations for the position. It's very important to ensure you are putting dollars and management attention toward hiring and developing best-in-class talent in the areas most critical to the client experience and thus to the long-term success of the business.

Question 5: Now that you've completed the matrix, what's next?

For those classified as "Wouldn't Hire Today," it's critical for the management team to determine what drives that classification. If the person works hard but is not a cultural fit because of the changes in the firm, the person still deserves respect for his or her efforts. If someone can't seem to get out of bed in the morning and get to the office on time or ignores client requests, it's a very different decision.

During transitions, leaders really do have to make sure they handle people in a way that enhances the culture regarding accountability that they are trying to build for the future. This may be especially true for those who are best in class. Without appropriate acknowledgment and rewards, you risk losing some of your most valuable assets. Most advisory practices are built on their human capital. We must invest in our staff as our form of research and development.

A central piece of the transition plan at Austin Asset was to create development plans for all employees, including the owners. These plans were designed to take one employee's individual role at the firm today and build a parallel path for that employee consistent with the strategic plan of the firm. Eric puts it this way: "It is great to have a plan to grow your firm, but will the employees grow along with the firm or will you have to hire replacement talent along the way?" Employees' development plans can focus on short-term personal and professional growth that feeds directly into the person you desire to have in three years. As time passes, you can assess the employee's actual personal development with the strategic plan of the business, making course corrections along the way to gauge how connected the strategic plan for the business is to the key ingredient in your client service offering, the firm's employees.

Improvement Matrix

The Supplemental Materials include an accountability matrix. As the successor takes over more of the daily activities of running the firm, processes and people will likely need to change. So much of the work used to be completed by the founder; as the founder is pulled away from the day-to-day activities, mistakes are going to happen. Using this matrix, a successor, along with the help of the others involved, can determine if the mistake was caused by:

- **Company Problem:** The firm is lacking a process to complete the task or the process is not designed properly. A good question to ask in this area is: If no matter whom I put in the situation would have failed, do I have a process problem? The answer is yes. If the transmission was put into a car where "R" actually meant forward, it doesn't matter who the driver is; the driver is going to fail.
- **Skills or experience:** In the transition process, people are going to be asked to get outside their comfort zone. It's important to assess if mistakes are being made because there's a lack of experience or a lack of training.
- **Execution Problem:** People can get by for long periods of time by going through the motions. However, there are many times when the process is sound, the training is sound, and a person just doesn't get the job done. That's fine in certain cases, as mistakes happen, but if someone continually doesn't meet your expectations, you have to question whether they should stay around.

Hire Slow. Fire Fast.
—Harvey Mackay

Emotions are often extremely high when it comes to keeping people or letting them go. However, don't make the mistake of taking people who are not really suitable for their roles and creating new roles for them unless it's obvious the organization needs those new positions. Do not forget the key items from earlier in this chapter. Assess the client service menu and experience. Assess the processes and roles needed to deliver on the goals of the company and those of the clients. Then decide on the right people to accomplish that. Doing the assessment in this order helps founders and successors focus clearly on the end result. People who don't really fit the process or delivery of the firm's goals for client service and business growth are simply not a fit for the firm.

The transition process can strengthen the culture of the business or it can fracture it. Nothing is riskier for the operational culture of a business than the way a firm decides to reward its people or let them go. Allowing underachievers to stay at the firm makes it difficult to raise the performance expectations for the business as a whole. Firing people too quickly or ungracefully can result in a gloom-and-doom environment for the new management team. But, done right, and with appropriate rewards for the "survivors" and with worthy new hires, an upgrading of the firm's people can set a very positive tone for future success.

KEY TAKEAWAYS:

1. The firm needs to determine whether it is simply replacing the founder with a successor and keeping the same processes and people or whether it is going to take the "road less traveled."
2. When assessing the operational aspects of the transition, a firm should always start from the viewpoint of the client. Once a firm determines the ideal client service experience, processes and people can be built toward achieving the desired experience.
3. Do not create new positions just to keep people who don't fit the longer-term goals for the business.
4. Few details are too small when it comes to the client communications and personal interaction during the transition.
5. If you get stuck making people decisions, use the framework set out in this chapter and in the Supplemental Materials.

Chapter 3

Ordering Off the Menu

By working faithfully eight hours a day you may eventually get to be the boss and work 12 hours a day.

—*Robert Frost*

In 2002, there was outrage by baseball purists when the All-Star game was called while the score was a tie. "There's no tie in baseball!" they cried. That's not true in business succession. Sometimes the best outcome is when neither side feels like they won. A tie is a compromise; instead of nobody winning, everybody wins.

There's a healthy tug-of-war going on during any transition. Founders can end up thinking they can accomplish whatever they want with no bad consequences because they started the business. Successors can also overestimate their importance, assuming they are owed more than they deserve. The right answer is usually somewhere in the middle. But where's the middle? Since this section of the book focuses on the operating issues, this permits us to emphasize the deep importance of the middle ground being what's best for the business, both in its day-to-day activities and for its long-term strategic success.

Choices Have Consequences

In talking to firms throughout the United States, regardless of geography, size, or client service model, we observe that founders want five things:

1. To maintain their current income level
2. To work fewer hours—or not at all
3. To maximize current enterprise value and retain equity upside
4. To maintain the independence of the firm
5. To find a successor or successor group

Some firms add a sixth item to this list, which is to leave a legacy. We'll deal with the concept of founder and successor legacy in Section III. As many of these firms are founder-centric, it is easy to see why some founders would believe they can "have their cake and eat it too." When these firms were founded, the needs of the business, the clients, and the founder were all absorbed within the same reality. As the business has grown, however, successors might feel that founders are blind to the changing needs of the firm. Founders often appear self-absorbed, even unreasonable. No good potential successor is going to stay at a firm for long where the needs of the founder are placed ahead of the needs of the business.

Most people don't go to breakfast and order French toast with a side of toast. The options on a menu tend to correlate, so once an individual chooses one thing they are unlikely to choose another. In the case of the founder's five- (or six-) item menu, of course, the tendency is to want to have everything; but making one choice generally makes other choices harder to achieve or even impossible. Many founders lack clarity in understanding these relationships.

We suggest founders determine the most important item on their list first. Achievement of all other choices on the menu can then build on the requirements of that most important objective. If a founder is at first not really sure, read on. The remainder of the chapter may be helpful, as we talk through various scenarios. Successors should do the same. The different—or congruent—preferences set the stage for an effective negotiation toward a good result.

This chapter sets up much of the important decision process we will explore in this book. The menu choices each party chooses have crucial ramifications for the financial and emotional aspects of the transition.

The Easiest One

We will start with the choice correlating with the least number of options. If a founder wants to maximize the short-term enterprise value of the firm (maximizing what financial value he or she gets up front) as the first priority, this part of the story is relatively easy. There are very important financial and emotional considerations to discuss later, but selling the business to an external third party is likely the best outcome for this objective. That sale option may come with installment arrangements and requirements for continued time commitments and compensation negotiations for continued employment, but the key related operational decision is the successor question. Does a successor increase or decrease your current enterprise value in the event of a sale? We believe that an increase in value is fairly obvious: continuity, new talents, new growth, and new energy. Some founders miss the intangible benefits of having a strong successor and how these intangibles impact valuations. When founders miss the point it's because they are looking at it myopically. They look at getting paid a multiple of profit and argue that the successor hurts the value of the business because of the compensation the successor receives. If a business will sell for six times free cash flow and a successor makes, say, $200,000 per year, some founders argue this means the enterprise value is decreased by $1,200,000. We believe that this is the wrong way to do the math. We dig much deeper into this topic in Section II.

The Great "Current Income" Debate

Founders of successful advisory businesses, certainly by average American income standards, enjoy very handsome levels of cash compensation. Founders of these businesses have worked hard to achieve their financial rewards and have usually developed an enviable standard of living. They usually have no intention of decreasing this standard as a result of the transition. Reasonable successors understand this desire, as they hope to be in the same position themselves as the business continues to enjoy success.

The current income menu choice is highly, and negatively, correlated with the "work fewer hours" choice. Founders generally need to choose one or the other as a primary focus, but often they want both and believe they can, somehow, get them. John Henry McDonald commented: "I started to leave gradually about five years ago. By 2013, I was just about out of the company but the coupons were really attractive. I couldn't easily give them up. I wanted a toe in the water. I had an expectation (unrealistic, I now realize) of being able to continue to collect large income from the firm but still working less and less. Eric keeps track of everything, including how much time I spent working. Eventually, he came to me and presented the facts: I was doing nothing *currently* for the firm but was still collecting big dollars. Eventually, it all worked out perfectly for me, thanks to Eric doing his job as CEO very well".

Jay contends, "There's nothing that has a bigger impact on the future of the business than the role the founder decides to play in the day-to-day activities of the firm and the cash compensation he or she receives for those efforts. A successor has to build around the operating style and demands of the founder. The founder had played a role and was performing work for the firm. If the founder no longer wants to do those activities, it costs money to replace that effort. I've been told by some founders that it's crazy to assume the budget for the replacement activities would come out of the founder's pocket. I think it's crazy to assume it would come from anywhere else. You deserve a payment for your ownership, but not as an employee unless you're actually doing some job."

If founders were to write their role description, most would say, "I do everything." This was probably the reality in the start-up and ramp-up stages of most advisory businesses. However, for a founder in transition, simply "I want to do less" is not an adequate role description. One of the hardest things for many successors is to get a founder to stick to a specific, limited role description and commit to high levels of performance in those activities within the business.

The debate over current income is a lot easier if the founder and successor are clear on where day-to-day responsibilities lie. Of course, the clients and staff benefit from this clarity as well.

How do founders and successors handle the discussion of roles and responsibilities? We've built a transition framework, which is included in the Supplemental Materials, on the principles of a basic "start," "stop," "continue" concept. Table 3.1 is an example of the framework filled in for a hypothetical transition.

Table 3.1   The Role Transition Framework

	Items Completed Today	Stop/Start/ Continue	When	To/From	Training Needed
Founder	Chair Investment Committee	Continue	For 1 year	Successor	Yes
	Meet with small prospects	Stop	Next 60 days	Founder	No
	Chair Advisory board	Start	Next 90 days	N/A	N/A
Successor	Meet with small prospects	Start	Next 60 days	Founder	No
	Train junior analysts	Stop	Next 90 days	Successor	Yes
	Attend meetings with founder	Continue	For 1 year	N/A	Yes

It is important that founders and successors understand what each other's responsibilities are for doing the day-to-day operations of the business throughout the transition. Founders and successors should build the framework as follows:

1. Start by laying out every important item you perform for the business.
2. Determine if you should stop doing it or continue doing it.
3. If you want to stop doing it, you should determine when and to whom you will assign the activity in the future. Also, an important component of this is to determine if the person you will transition the activity to is really well suited to do it. If training is needed, training may need to start immediately to meet the transition timeline.
4. If you want to continue doing the task, determine for how much longer. These activities should tie in to the overall transition plan. If the founder wants to be completely out of the business in six months, it's not ideal for him or her to be the only person making investment decisions three months before departure.

This framework gives founders and successors a visual representation to discuss any material changes to job responsibilities. If there are material changes, the current income debate is likely to be more of an issue. Another suggestion is to have the successor and the founder sit down and work on a document around the strengths of the founder. This gives the successor a chance to reflect on the strengths on which the business was built. If the successor can clearly articulate the strengths of the founder, it celebrates the founder's achievements but also leads to a way to discuss the changes that may need to occur to transition the roles (and, ultimately, income) appropriately. In Section II we will drill more deeply into the financial issue of separating reward for labor from reward for ownership.

Equity versus "Milking"

As we review in the financial chapters of this book, a firm's ability to be sold may have an impact on an owner's cash vs. equity decision. Maximizing current cash flow in most cases has longer-term ramifications. Let's start with the client responsibility aspect of this decision. Many founders, after looking at all scenarios, determine that internal succession or selling the business are not options they are willing to execute. They have great lifestyles. They don't have to work that hard. They aren't going to get what they believe the business is worth in a sale event. So what's left for them to do? They are left with the option of "milking" the business for cash flow. This means they solve for the amount of annual cash they can take out of the business while still permitting it to operate ... for a while. The firm runs lean and is extremely profitable. The firm invests the minimum amount possible in people and technology, and invests little in its own future. This strategy, however, no longer solves for equity value, and the firm will likely have little if any equity value once the founder eventually has to leave the business due to death or infirmity. The challenge we see here is in the common benchmarking that focuses on highly profitable firms as exhibiting a "best practice" from a financial view. That view risks the operational shortsightedness of "excessive" profit.

This "milking" approach draws little respect from most people, including those founders who are willing to judge it. Still, many seem to have moved clearly onto that plan and sit at industry conferences proud of large profit margins and the amount of income they take out of the business. As we have emphasized, the client has to be at the center of the transition. If that's the case, it is difficult to see how the "milking" strategy benefits clients. Some may not agree with our opinion here, but unless this strategy is executed in some transparent way, how is this fair to the clients? And if it's not transparent, it's almost a fraud perpetrated on those clients. As Jay summarizes it: "You make an explicit, or at least implicit, promise to clients that their interests come first. If you aren't investing in the business and its people, you are breaching that promise."

What Does a Successor Want off the Menu

In all advisory businesses, the retirements of the Baby Boomers are causing a war for talent. In the financial services industry alone, according to Cerulli's Advisor Metrics Quantitative Update 2013, by 2020 there will be a shortage of 50,000 financial advisors. Take this shortage for advisors alone and factor in that only a fraction of advisors are actually able to help manage and run firms, and it's easy to see why good successors will be in high demand.

This factual reality is key for founders to understand. They aren't the only ones ordering off the menu, and the choices a founder makes impact whether or not he or she will be able to cultivate an appropriate successor. Eric is surprised when he attends conferences and hears people wonder why they don't have younger talent in the firm. His next question is about ownership. "I understand why most firms are still tightly controlled, but some owners think it's inspiring to own just 1 percent of a firm. Why would any good successor get excited by that level of ownership?"

In talking to most reasonable successors, we are not surprised by what they want from their menu of choices:

1. They want a founder to be clear about what he or she is willing to do and not do, in the daily operations of the business, with a clear understanding of how management control will work today and into the future.

2. They want the vision and mission of the firm to remain focused on service to the client and also to celebrate the legacy of the founder. But the celebration of legacy cannot get in the way of making the changes needed to better serve a client.

3. They want to understand how they become a larger owner of the firm based on a fair valuation and a realistic acquisition process and time frame.

4. They want the current income for the founder to be fair based on day-to-day role and ownership. This current income calculation also needs to be fair for the proper reinvestment into the firm.

5. They want the current owner(s) to understand the financial constraints that may be present, understanding the creative structures that might need to be in place so a successor can afford to buy.

6. They expect an appropriately large percentage of the upside in the business valuation.

Not Everyone Is William Wallace

As we discussed in Chapter 1, many founders fought hard to gain their independence and build their own firms. This desire for independence remains at many advisory firms, and many founders feel this is an important choice off the menu. We picture founders like William Wallace (Mel Gibson in the movie *Braveheart*), fighting to gain their freedom and then fighting to keep it. However, founders often miss two very important points around independence. Founders have said to us: "If I sell the business, my employees will lose their independence. Why don't they understand that and want to work harder or buy ownership to keep the firm the way it is?" Most founders are like William Wallace; most employees are not. In even the most disaggregated ownership model, relatively few employees of the overall employee base will likely be owners. Those relatively many nonowners aren't "independent" now. Working for someone else won't be very different.

Founders tend to say they want to remain independent as a key variable but are unwilling to dispense with other menu items. According to Bernie Clark, "Per our Schwab data, 70 percent of firms say they want to be 'legacy' firms, but most haven't really done anything yet to accomplish that. Transitioning from a 'lifestyle' firm to a durable business will be necessary, but, for many, it's not really desirable." Remaining independent or building a legacy requires the players on the field to sacrifice other items on the menu to achieve this goal.

If remaining independent or building a legacy is your most important menu choice, there are two questions to answer: Do I have a team in place to sustain the business for the next 20 years? If I don't, what am I willing to do and give up to put that team in place? Don't just answer the second question with a vague statement. Get specific. What amount of equity would you give to the future team? What percentage of current income are you willing to reinvest? How much time each week are you going to dedicate to the effort of finding the right team?

Determining what each party wants in the transition of a firm is crucial. We continue to revisit these topics throughout the remaining sections of the book.

KEY TAKEAWAYS:

1. There is a menu of choices throughout the transition process. You can't have every item.
2. The items on the menu correlate. Founders and successors must choose one or two "deal breakers" and let the remaining items fall out from there.
3. To adequately deal with the "current income" debate, successors and founders need to be clear about their current and future roles in the daily operations of the business.
4. "Milking" the business rarely serves the best interests of clients.
5. Most firms claim to want to leave a legacy and remain independent but have not taken the necessary steps to achieve these goals.

Chapter 4

Setting a Vision, Together

Perfection is not attainable, but if we chase perfection we can catch excellence.

—*Vince Lombardi*

Identifying a successor and strategizing the future of the business is the hardest and most important decision a founder will ever make. The stakes are nearly as high for a successor. A decision on which firm and founder to tie their future to is probably the most important career decision successors can make. Given the very high stakes, it's important to understand the challenges and opportunities here. Getting this wrong on either side can impair career paths, deteriorate client relationships, and, ultimately, diminish the equity value of the firm.

This chapter comes just before we start the financial section of the book. This is no accident, largely owing to a discussion with Mark Tibergien. After seeing many firm transitions, his main cautionary note was a simple one: "In advisory services, if you haven't reconciled what the client succession plan is going to be and what the management succession is going to be, then there's no way you can resolve the economic (equity succession) question." Firms can't have a client succession plan without a management succession plan. And the equity succession plan that sits alongside these can be either deliberately compatible with them or deliberately of its own design and at its own pace. In any case, for many firms it feels like a chicken-and-egg conundrum. Where do you start? Does it matter? We're convinced that you shouldn't start with the money.

During the transition process, the founder and successor have two hurdles to jump that circle around each other. If the founder and successor can't work together, the transition isn't going to work. How do founders and successors determine if they can work together? Most of the time it's best to determine a shared vision for the business. This can be an effective, iterative path to good conclusions or it can become a circular nightmare. (See Figure 4.1.)

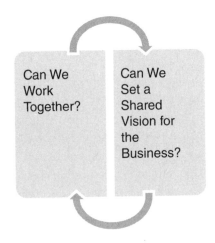

Figure 4.1   Alignment Hurdle

STEP 1: Can We Work Together?

Personality Matters

> Always be yourself, express yourself, have faith in yourself, do
> not go out and look for a successful personality and duplicate it.
>
> —*Bruce Lee*

Founders and successors need to be themselves throughout this process. It may seem right to try to appease the other side, avoid conflict, and hope the process ends well. But it doesn't matter what the rest of the transition looks like ... it doesn't matter if the money works ... it doesn't matter if the business plan is the best ever seen ... it doesn't matter if the people in transition are already closely linked as family members. If the founder and successor can't enjoy being around each other, the transition will likely fail. Personality profiling systems and compatibility tests may play a role here, but we believe there are some practical things a founder and successor should think about—and do. Chapter 2 explored the importance of understanding differences. The founder and successor having different and complementary strengths can build a strong foundation for a business. But are there some personality differences that might impede the business transition?

Is it important for us to spend time outside of work together?

Ed McMahon and Johnny Carson served as one of this country's longest-running comedy teams. In his book *Here's Johnny: My Memories of Johnny Carson, The Tonight Show, and 46 Years of Friendship* (Rutledge Hill Press, 2005), McMahon talks about his relationship with Carson and how it was different from that of most comedic teams: "Most comic teams are not good friends or even friends at all. Laurel and Hardy didn't hang out together, Abbott and Costello weren't best of friends. Johnny and I were the happy exception. For 40 years Johnny and I were as close as two non-married people can be. And if he heard me say that, he might say, 'Ed, I always felt you were my insignificant other.' "

Teammates operate successfully when they complement each other in their respective roles, deploying their respective talents, not necessarily because they are friends. However, some people feel that a genuine closeness among business partners is necessary. Determining what style is important to you and your counterpart is important.

The differing opinions and styles of the authors of this book show why this is important. Jay feels it's important to have a relationship built not only on the office but outside it as well. "I don't expect my business partners to be my best friends. That's not likely to happen and maybe not a good thing to be that close, anyway. However, I do want my business partners to be people I enjoy grabbing a beer with after work from time to time."

Eric doesn't feel spending time together outside the office in the longer term is important, but it certainly is in the beginning. Eric spent a lot of time with John Henry in his early years at the company. Eric jokes, "I was kind of like his shadow. I would just follow him around. I'd listen and learn. This included inside the office and outside." Eric didn't have any kids at the time, so on Saturdays he would help John Henry with landscaping and other things, since they enjoyed each other's company. However, Eric eventually did have kids and developed different interests, so they began to spend less time together. "It went from a relationship where we liked each other personally and enjoyed spending time together, to a situation where we respect and appreciate how we each take care of the business. This change wasn't a bad thing. It was just the reality of the age gap in our lives and interests." John Henry describes their relationship: "It was not a love affair … certainly not at the beginning, but it developed into a mutual respect. It was not a matter of the heart, but of the mind."

A clear differentiator of the founder–successor relationship and the successor–team relationship is that after a successor has been chosen, it *is* important for that person to become closer to his/her team. In Eric's case, as his relatively close relationship with John Henry waned, it was critical for him to enhance those connections with his new partners-to-be. These new partners had been on the team for years as strong employees. The future success of the firm, and completion of the transition plan, hinged on their roles changing from employees to owners/leaders. He couldn't orchestrate this on his own, nor did he want to. In one case the common factor was a love of automobiles and in another case it was an appreciation for the game of golf. These bonds made the transition from the founder easier because some other members of the staff might be his successors someday. Eric and his new partners built stronger relationships because they had a new, shared fate. John Henry alone became less crucial to the future success of the firm. All of them together became more crucial to that success.

Tim's relationship with Rob Francais was always one of respect and admiration, but it was not in either of their personalities or life patterns to become personally close. There was a 20-year age difference, Rob had young children while Tim had none, and their homes were 400 miles apart. But both had led firms with very strong internal friendship bonds, and they shared a vision for their combination into Aspiriant to achieve great results for all their constituencies—most significantly with their friends and colleagues at Kochis Fitz and Quintile near the top of the list. A good analogy might be that they combined two families—without getting married to each other.

Does the successor expect the founder to be a mentor? Is the founder aligned with this vision?

Founders and successors are likely to be at different phases in life. The experience of the founder is invaluable to the next generation. A question Jay hears frequently as he visits firms is: Do successors want to be mentored? "If you have a successor and he doesn't want to be mentored, you haven't identified the right successor. If you are the successor and you don't think there's something you can learn from the founder, you need to move on." As Eric puts it, "When the student shows up, so must the teacher. If this isn't happening, one or the other—or both—haven't shown up."

Certainly the mentoring relationship can change over time. It also depends on the size of the firm. In Austin Asset's situation, there was one founder (John Henry) and one identified successor (Eric). Eric saw John Henry as a mentor early in their relationship. Since John Henry did not have children, Eric felt like a surrogate adopted son. He eventually got to a point where he needed a different kind of mentorship. Eric started building out his own list of mentors. There were things John Henry couldn't offer anymore. This changed their relationship, both from a personal and from a partnership standpoint. It was an emotional challenge, but the change was for the better. As Eric grew in his position at the company and found outside mentors, he felt John Henry started to take him much more seriously as a leader for the company.

Like a child leaving home for college, Eric was becoming his own man. It's often at that point that children first realize a changed dynamic between themselves and their parents. Parents have a foundational history. They see their children along a continuum, including the children's limitations, defined by their view of them as younger people who need protection. In college, kids often align themselves with a professor or a coach who doesn't have this limiting historical view. This absence of historical framing permits a new mentor to encourage students to escape self-imposed limitations and envision wholly new possibilities. Similarly, the mentoring relationships a successor has, not only with the founder but also with those sources of perspective and coaching outside the firm's staff structure, can significantly benefit the firm. Those external mentors might be others in the same industry or contacts from other lines of business or other professions; they might also be, and frequently are, clients. Who better to have insight into the firm's strengths and weaknesses? Who better to benefit from the development of successor talent?

In the case of larger firms, the mentor–mentee relationship may not be a straightforward, one-to-one relationship. It may be more of a mutually supportive, developmental web. Still, the requirement that the future learn from the past is at work in larger firms, and founders and their successors still encounter the same interpersonal dynamic.

How do I prefer to communicate? How do I prefer people to communicate with me?

There are great communicators, average communicators, and poor communicators. There are people who are promptly and thoroughly responsive, and those who are not. Being toward the excellent end of this scale is helpful; but it's even more important that founders and successors understand the differences in their respective learning and communication styles. So much effective communication is lost when the parties involved don't realize they are, in effect, speaking different languages, through different media. Many people use elaborate personality and communication analyses to get a grip on this reality. We applaud those techniques and encourage people to learn more. But we recommend boiling things down to something quite simple: There are readers, and there are listeners. Readers prefer written communication. Listeners prefer direct interaction. Don't underestimate the problems that can result from failing to understand this simple framework during leadership transitions.

Jay is a listener. "I've worked for 'readers' and it drives me crazy," he explains. "To me, it seems such a waste of time to write long e-mails to each other over business decisions which can be made in a 30-second conversation. I think some of it comes from my impatience." Eric is a reader. "I like to get something in writing," he says, "because it gives me a chance to reread it."

Successors can find it difficult to deal with the communication issues caused by workload inequality. As some founders choose to slow down, work fewer hours, and lessen client and management responsibilities, they sometimes "roam" the office, still wanting to keep a personal relationship with the successor and others within the company. Eric had to come up with an "I'm in the zone" signal to John Henry. When Eric was working "in the zone," he asked John Henry to respect the momentum of the work and give him some space until he was ready to talk about other things. Asking John Henry to give Eric something to read and ponder in the meantime was sometimes really helpful.

Expectations for Accessibility

Founders in the transition process are found on both ends of a spectrum running from micromanagers to "absentee owners." Of course, some founders are in the middle of that spectrum, but the micromanager and absentee owners tend to dominate the accessibility landscape. The successor needs rules of engagement for each type.

Let's tackle the "absentee" founder first: In the transition process, founders often want to spend more time out of the office. However, during this period some successors still need the founder's input on major client or internal issues, so the founder needs to be accessible. This should be a rare situation, as the successor should be self-sustaining, but issues can come up. Without rules of engagement, a successor can be put in a tough position. If the successor can't engage with the founder because the founder is on a three-week cruise and not returning phone calls, it's an issue. Successors should get founder buy-in on how to engage on major issues and agree on what defines a major issue. Founders have earned the right to get away, and their being away allows the successors to grow. Rules of engagement benefit the founder as much as the successor, but firms need to be intentional about it.

When Tim stepped down as CEO of Aspiriant, he took a pre-announced six-month sabbatical. This was designed to facilitate Tim's complete absence from the firm for a long enough period of time to give Rob Francais an unimpeded avenue from which to exert his authority as the new CEO. Tim's e-mail account and voice mail were shut down. There was a midpoint telephone conversation scheduled, and each party knew how to reach the other in an emergency; otherwise, being "incommunicado" was the deliberate plan.

At the other extreme, a micromanager founder can sap the energy of the successor and risks confusing other staff about who really is in charge. In talking to successors, a common reaction to a micromanaging founder is: "If you need me to ask you about everything or you want to sit in my office all day and watch me work, you need to get a life. If you want to do it yourself, you don't need me. We need to rethink this whole transition process. This isn't working!"

Solving this problem requires the successor to be proactive. Try using one of the following two frameworks, or both of them.

The first, Figure 4.2, is inspired by Stephen Covey's *The 7 Habits of Highly Effective People*. It is designed to look at items/tasks/situations at the intersection of important and urgent. "Important" is defined by its impact on the business. "Urgent" is defined by its time sensitivity.

Eric lays out what would be his rules of engagement: "I want complete access, going both ways, between founder and successor on the top left quadrant. I want agreement to a weekly meeting to deal with 'important but not urgent.' Neither founders nor successors should be dealing directly with the other two categories."

We'll call the second framework the "micromanager killer." Micromanagers are terrible delegators. When you are lucky enough to get a micromanager who appears to delegate responsibility, the experience can be painful when the delegator can't really give up detailed involvement. The goal, then, is to arm a successor for his or her proactive assertion

	Urgent	Not Urgent
Important	* Trade error * Client death * IRS Audit announced * SEC surprise audit * Judge announces decision	* Taking a client out to lunch * Newsletter theme months away * Building relationship with new employee
Not Important	* Minor employee issue * Interruption in your office * Pointless meeting	* Spam e-mails * Watching television * Responding to someone always creating fires

Figure 4.2   Priority Matrix

of authority to increase the delegation of work and lower frustration on both sides.

Identify what should be delegated. As a successor, you very often need to take the lead in getting a founder to delegate. Make three lists. The first lists those items/tasks you believe you are very good at performing (ideally, items you also enjoy performing). The second list includes items the founder performs today but either dislikes or isn't really very good at doing. The third list contains the items most important to the business. Then take these lists and find commonalities, creating a three-circle Venn diagram, as illustrated by Figure 4.3.

Figure 4.3   Delegation Diagram

The intersection of any two, but especially all three, of these lists identifies the items that should be more effectively delegated. If the founder is honest about his or her dislikes, this will be liberating. Areas for candid negotiation remain—where the parties have differing views of their respective competencies. But at least it's a start.

Create rules of engagement. Once you have a final list (maybe long, but often fairly short) of items the successor has pried from the hands of the founder, an ongoing understanding about communication is key. We suggest founders and successors put the delegated responsibilities into three categories.

1. **Ready, aim, fire:** These are items where the founder expects a plan to be in place and reviewed with the founder before the successor begins execution. The founder and successor agree on the major architecture of a strategy with the successor, then executing its details and reporting back to the founder on the results along the way. Those periodic reports keep the project from veering too far from the original intent but still give the successor plenty of discretion in reaching the next milestone.
2. **Keep me posted:** This category requires no specific plan or even discussion up front. The successor sets both the target and the path to achieve it, but reports back to the founder periodically on progress or even after the item is completed. The objective here is not to encourage the founder to "second-guess," but to prevent the founder from being "out of the loop."
3. **Bermuda Triangle:** These are items the successor has full authority to handle however they choose. The founder just wants them to disappear. At first, these tend to be very low-risk items or items whose outcome isn't irrevocable.

Successors can use this framework to give themselves confidence in creating the rules of communication and responsibility engagement. Ultimately, if the succession transition is to succeed at all, the firm will likely operate more effectively if successors take this lead and if founders are open to relinquishing that leadership. But this exercise is meant to be fluid. As respect and confidence in the relationship grows, there are fewer items in the "Ready, Aim, Fire" category and more in the "Bermuda Triangle."

Recognize and Agree on When You Do Your Best Work

This may sound trivial, but it wouldn't be in the book if we thought it was unimportant. It is helpful to talk about expectations about work patterns—not only how many hours a day or how many days a week but at what time of day. Morning people enjoy being up and active before others are fully engaged. Night owls often get a "second wind" when others have already fully disengaged from the workday. Each of these types of people is happy being productive with relatively few distractions from face-to-face, interpersonal demands. Still others function best only when energized by the hustle and bustle of lots of interaction. Understanding when you and your counterpart do your best work can result in enhanced work patterns and complementary project responsibility. Maybe the biggest benefit is the greater respect and appreciation for ways of getting things done that differ from your own.

How Will Disagreements Be Settled?

Mike Tyson, heavyweight champion boxer, once famously said: "Everyone has a plan, until they get punched in the face." Even the success stories we chronicle had rocky periods. The most successful transitions are not linear: problems occur and unexpected obstacles arise; under the best of circumstances, you won't agree on everything. If founders and successors start from this understanding, they can plan, up front, how they'll overcome at least some of the hurdles.

Wayne Gretzky, hailed as one of the greatest hockey players of all time, urged that success relied not on skating to where the puck is but on skating to where it's going to be. As a successor, think of where you *want* that puck to be and skate there. Some conflict is inevitable. You are not in charge of the business—at least not yet. You didn't found the business. You may be on the verge of signing some type of longer-term deal—either laying out cash, taking on debt, or earning illiquid sweat equity in the business, and maybe all of these. You have a lot at stake, and you are not in complete control. Jay cautions, "As a successor, at some point you will do battle with the founder. It would be a smart idea to understand what types of weapons you have to use and what type of army you have with you if it comes to that. The easiest way to fight a battle is to have truce terms already in place before the war begins."

Standard negotiating tactics apply, of course. Be certain of your "no fallback position": what you are absolutely not going to give in on. Anything better than that is a win for you and probably produces a win for the founder as well. That's the goal of any successful resolution: both sides perceiving that they've come away with something better than their own absolute minimum—a win-win.

Eric offers this: "As we started our transition process, I wrote down an actual list of "deal breakers," those items that were critical to success from my perspective, and treated them as foundational for where I planned/hoped the process would take us."

Can a "third-party" resolution process help? Maybe. Eric has an interesting take on this issue. In the beginning he and John Henry had an advisory board. The advisory board members, although they did not serve a formal governance role, assisted in the transition when the two of them developed a conflict. The board was really created as a "second set of eyes." Eric elaborates, "The advisory board helped keep us focused on the business results and kept us from singing our own praises ... right into the ditch. It wasn't about what was good for either of us, individually; it was about what was good for the business." Over time, Eric saw the role of the advisory board become less important in the conflict resolution part of the business. "We were taking the long view. This meant decisions we were making didn't have an immediate impact on the business. However, as John Henry saw the growth come and the profitability increase, many of the disagreements just melted away."

We caution successors to be careful about relying too heavily on support from these kinds of actual or quasi-governing systems. Advisory boards can work extremely well. However, don't fool yourself into thinking they have more power than they do. Even if your firm has a formal, fiduciary governing board, the majority control within it is all that matters, and if that majority is controlled by the founder it can be even worse than no board at all. The appearance of an independent, confirming authority puts even more weight behind the founder's position. Controlling the majority has its perks.

Who Will Set the Priorities?

We've heard entrepreneurs described as human popcorn machines, popping out new ideas at every turn. For a successor, this is exciting and challenging. However, when the popcorn machines are spending most of their time in client and prospect meetings and other daily chores of running the business, there's little time to pop out new ideas. One of the benefits of a successful transition process is freeing up more of that creative talent. The sheer number of ideas can be overwhelming. Google the final scene of the movie *Real Genius,* which stars Val Kilmer, to better understand what it feels like to be a successor with a fully functioning popcorn machine.

There are emotional issues involved in setting company priorities, which we address at length in Section III. Here, we merely introduce some important techniques for setting priorities. Eric describes one approach: "In the beginning I would waste a lot of time. I wanted to be respectful to John Henry, but he had a new idea every day and it was hard to stay focused on what he really wanted me to work on. I finally started ignoring the ideas until he brought them up a second time. If he mentioned it a second time, I would believe he was serious and ask him if this was something he wanted me to spend time on. That's probably not the best approach, but it's the best I could come up with at the time."

We suggest successors come up with a monthly or quarterly priority process. Then include everyone who is relevant in this process. Allow even the entire company to weigh in on what they think should be the priorities of the next month or quarter. Part of a successor's role is to provide structure where before there may have been little. Having all the right people involved at the front end and participating in discussions of why items were chosen makes all of them feel better about what was chosen and better aligns their individual efforts with the priorities of the company. A successor needs to try to establish rules with the founder about abrupt changes of course or too many new initiatives. Such things should only happen infrequently and have a compelling business reason. They can't be flavors of the month.

We all learned at some fairly early point in our lives about opportunity costs. If we spent our allowance on some new toy, we couldn't enjoy as many ice cream cones. All choices have consequences, including the choices we do not make. Spinning the wheels of the organization during the transition because priorities are not clear is potentially a huge waste for all parties. Founders and successors—and the business itself—all benefit from a clear set of priorities and a steady focus on actually achieving them.

Step 2: Setting a Vision

Buying into a business ultimately requires a leap of faith. Putting all of the other issues to one side, a transition is going to get to a point where a founder and successor have to be "all in." The founder is going to be betting his or her retirement lifestyle, or philanthropic wherewithal, or psychic legacy—or all three—on the future success of the business. The successor is going to be betting his or her family's financial goals and professional career on this same business. When going "all in," it's good to know if you are holding a pair of aces or a pair of twos. How do you know?

To create a shared vision, the founder and successor need to ask themselves five key questions, more or less in sequence, as shown in Figure 4.4.

Creating Culture

In his 2011 groundbreaking book *Grow,* Jim Stengel lays out compelling results of a 10-year brand study: "The latest research, including a 10-year growth study I conducted of more than 50,000 brands around the world, has inspired and validated this new framework. The world's

Figure 4.4   Shared Vision Sequence

best businesses achieve growth three times or more than that of the competition in their categories. The central principle of the new framework is the importance of having a brand ideal, a shared goal of improving people's lives. A brand ideal is a business's essential reason for being, the higher order benefit it brings to the world. A brand ideal of improving people's lives is the only sustainable way to recruit, unite, and inspire all the people a business touches, from employees to customers. It is the only thing that enduringly connects the core beliefs of the people inside a business with the fundamental human values of the people the business serves. Without the connection, without a brand ideal, no business can truly excel."

The top brands are about improving people's lives. Based on this premise, an advisory business has a built-in advantage. This improving people's lives premise is what founders built their firms around. As we discussed in Chapter 1, most founders started advisory businesses because they believed their former models were broken and that their clients deserved better. How do founders and successors continue this ideal throughout the transition and beyond? The first step is to talk about it.

What does your firm stand for now and into the future? Anne Shumadine, cofounder of Signature, one of the first multifamily offices founded in the United States, speaks about the fluidity a firm needs to be successful. However, she expects the foundational principles the firm was built on to remain the same. One of these cultural tenets for Signature was to downplay the importance of individuals for the betterment of the team: "We have always wanted Signature to be an institution. From day one, we downplayed the founders and individual performers. We always wanted clients to rely on the company and not on the person."

An ideal drives culture. Culture is created top down, not bottom up. Still many founders acknowledge that their best intellectual skill resides in being able to synthesize and operationalize the values and visions that originate from others. In any event, the founder drove the culture when he or she started the firm. The culture of the firm's future will then be driven by the successor, its new champion, but must still be supported by the founder as they together accomplish their transition. And the really foundational principles of the firm are likely to remain paramount. Those are likely what clients and staff respect the most. So they are probably the most powerful foundation for future success.

Founders and successors also need to understand that the firm's culture is being reinforced—or dissipated—by the way they go through the transition process itself. Eric Kittner, a successor partner at Moneta Group, describes himself not as a successor but as a "continuity plan." "I don't like the successor term because it leads to the assumption that this is the end. This is only the beginning. I want someone to want to come behind me and I need to set the stage for that person by the way I treat my [founding] partner Joe as he exits the business."

However, culture also exhibits itself in many small details, which in isolation may seem unimportant but cumulatively have major ramifications for the business. Do we allow summer hours for employees? How are we going to handle remote employees? What is our social media policy? What is the dress code? Some of these are generationally sensitive issues. Many firms will first address these issues only at the time of transition. Getting those elements of culture right can support a successful transition. A poor transition can leave many of these questions still unanswered, to the possible confusion and frustration of staff and clients.

This is a chance for the founder and successor to engage the whole firm in a "should/could" exercise. Eric notes that one of the things that was hard for him with John Henry was that the firm was so much John Henry's creation and its values were so much John Henry's values. The team was told what those values were, as opposed to the values being built from the ground up. "From my view," explains Eric, "I wanted to embrace the team to take a fresh look at these items together, so their feedback was included and made part of the story. I did one-on-one meetings with each employee during the month after John Henry's retirement to discuss "what the firm should be *and* what the firm could be. I was clear with each of them that this was a blank slate on which to dream and imagine how they saw the firm. Little did I know how amazing the feedback would be—some affirming, some challenging, and all of it truly valuable. If a founder and successor could go through this together, with their team, on the front end, it would be a great tool for them to build the firm's going-forward vision."

Setting Growth Goals

We believe there is an absence of self-reflection at many firms and that the transition process can shine light on a firm's true colors. Everyone walks into the planning process and says they want to grow. However, so many firms are kidding themselves. Many founders are happy with what they have. They may not need the firm to grow to meet their goals; but for the successor to meet his or her goals, the firm definitely needs to grow. Successors really need to take this topic seriously. Successors need to figure out whether they are willing to make the sacrifices needed to grow. If the answer is "yes," successors better next ensure that the people around them are also willing to make the same sacrifices.

The Right Client and Service Menu—Driving Value

We will devote the next section of this book primarily to financial issues, discussing at length what drives equity valuations. The biggest determinants of value are the characteristics of the client base, its durability, and its growth rate. Firms successfully transitioning management control and equity ownership strive to put the client at the center. The client needs to be at the center of a vision built by the successor and the founder. The clients the firm desires to serve, in the ways the firm is prepared to be excellent, drive everything: the service menu, necessary employee skill sets, and the desired client experience.

What type of client does the firm wish to serve over the next five or 10 years? What clients will value the type of firm its leaders desire to maintain or to build? This is an especially difficult question today. Regardless of the particular business model within the advisory services industry, technology and demographic changes are causing major challenges to how a firm produces value. In the financial advisory space, "robo advisors"(algorithmic money management platforms, sometimes accessible at very little cost, even as mobile apps on smart phones) are gaining market share with a younger client base. In the accounting realm, the commoditization of tax return preparation and other compliance services is picking up speed. In the legal world, some firms are moving to fixed-fee engagements, as opposed to open-ended hourly rates. No firm can safely plan to stand still.

Building the Right Team

In Chapter 2, we reviewed a framework for the "people" component. We encourage you to revisit that discussion. Having a shared vision helps founders and successors understand in which direction to aim the bus. The last step of the shared vision process is to determine whether the right people are on that bus.

We'll address these issues and more as we look at the financial dimensions of transition and succession in Section II.

KEY TAKEAWAYS:

1. The transition process has an operational dynamic that causes a push and pull between the personality differences of the founder and the successor and the need to define a shared vision of the future of the business.
2. That shared vision of the future needs to be grounded on an ideal—what the firm wants to stand for now and into the future.
3. Founders and successors need to ask themselves the key questions in this process around five core areas: culture, growth, client profile, service menu, and employees.
4. The future vision of the firm cannot be formed just by the founders or by the successors. The vision needs to be a combination of their visions and those of other key stakeholders—especially the clients.
5. Without a prioritization process, founders and successors will waste time and energy on projects that do not drive strategic value.

Section II

FINANCIAL CHALLENGES ... AND SOLUTIONS

Chapter 5

It's Always About the Money

Money has never made man happy, nor will it, there is nothing in its nature to produce happiness. The more of it one has, the more one wants.

—*Benjamin Franklin*

In Section I, we reviewed the importance of having a clear vision for the future of the firm, understanding what is best for the firm and its clients. If you are a founder or a successor and this isn't yet clear to you, go back and do your homework. Seriously. Mark Tibergien lays out the pitfalls if you don't: "The error people make in this process is to mistake genuine succession for mere equity transition. As soon as the financial issues get put first, people end up looking for a deal." Going right to the economics means neither side can close the gap. There's not enough positive emotional investment to counterweight the emotional obstacles. Whatever a successor offers appears to diminish the founder, and the successor believes that the founder is coming from a position of greed. Feelings are capable of being hurt on all sides. Our goal in this section of the book is not to get "into the weeds" on deal dynamics, financial statement reviews, or other factors that appropriately influence the ultimate transaction. Rather, our goal is to show how the intersection of the financial dimension with the organizational and emotional dimensions can produce challenges—that can be overcome.

In this chapter, we take a big-picture view, and then we drill deeper into these issues in Chapters 6 and 7.

As we researched material for this book, we interviewed 26 founders, successors, consultants, and long-tenured industry observers. We started every conversation with the same question: "What do you think is the most important item a firm must overcome to be successful in the transition of ownership and management control?" We were lucky to have extremely smart, articulate, accomplished, and insightful people willing to collaborate in answering that question. Not surprisingly, we received many different answers. In contrast to Tibergien's viewpoint, for example, Charles Goldman didn't hesitate to assert that he believes it's about the financial aspects. "Transitions are built like Maslow's pyramid of the hierarchy of needs. Just as clients need to be at the center of any transition plan, the financial aspects need to be dealt with as early as possible because they are the 'survival' component for the players involved. Only after the financial aspects are satisfied can you effectively address the self-esteem and emotional issues. I think the financial aspect is the most difficult item to solve and so far in the advisory industry, unfortunately, only rarely has it been solved."

Most advisory businesses have a direct (or at least a strong indirect) involvement in advising clients in some aspect of their financial health. Certified public accounting (CPA) firms do sophisticated tax planning, money managers help clients establish investment strategies and attempt to generate returns, wealth managers do that and develop and implement clients' financial plans as well, and attorneys craft sophisticated estate plans. If so many advisory businesses touch so many aspects of clients' financial health, why do they need to be schooled in the fundamentals of finance for their own activities? The obvious answer is their lack of objectivity and dispassion when it comes to their own circumstances. As Rob Francais jokes, "Technically, the financial terms of transition should be easy. We all know the rules and we're all comfortable with the analytics. Once we agree that the price should be \$X, we can transfer anything to anybody for that \$X and call it a day." Of course, it's not that easy. There are deep emotional issues tied to both the result and the process of getting to that \$X.

An Ironic Twist

In Chapter 1, we talked about the founding of the independent advisory space. Many founders left relatively comfortable employment positions and went out on their own, largely to solve for what was best for their clients and have a large ownership stake in what they were building. Rob Francais points out the ironic twist of what has happened. "There are two models: an employee model and an ownership model. Founders of independent firms left the employee model to start their own firms and replaced it with the ownership model where there was a complete alignment of interest between owner, employee, and client. Now as those firms have grown, many founders want to continue to own a very large share of their firms, maintain control, but still have successors. However, those successors are right back into the employee model. For a firm to remain independent and do what's best for its clients, the ownership model needs to prevail to retain the alignment of interests that worked so well in the beginning."

Rob's point is an interesting one. In the beginning of most independent advisory firms, the fact that management control and equity ownership were consolidated in the founder was a good thing. The founder was on the front lines serving clients. The founder was doing what was best for the client, growing the business by doing so, and reaping the financial rewards from being focused on the clients' welfare. However, as founders step back from the day-to-day operations of the business and the service of clients, a divergence can emerge between what is best for the client and what appears to those founders as best for their personal interest in the financial performance of the firm. This potential divide cannot be ignored.

If the advisory space stays employment based versus ownership based, it will be difficult for many firms to remain independent. David DeVoe, head of DeVoe & Company, a consulting business focused on equity transitions within the advisory business, believes that if this divergence continues, firms that do not widen ownership to future generations will be in trouble. "Eventually, good potential successors will vote with their feet and leave. I believe that unless the owners of firms begin to do something about widening ownership, successor departures will increase."

Management versus Equity

An important part of the transition difficulties advisory businesses face is confusion around the concepts of ownership, value, management authority, and control. We have long believed that it is essential to conceptually separate "ownership" of the firm, the equity, from the firm's "management." Equity is about the concentration or distribution of value. Its defining features are access to the firm's net earnings and, maybe someday, the proceeds of a sale, and, of course, an ultimate level of control. Ownership is a status. It can't be taken away; it is just bought and sold. Management, on the other hand, is about the concentration or distribution of power. Its defining features are competence, performance, and accountability. None of these personal characteristics or behaviors are necessary to the status of ownership, but, one hopes, they are always found in management. Management is a job. It can't be bought or sold. Success in a job should bring additional rewards; failure in a job should lead to being fired—from that job.

The earlier this distinction takes hold, the better organized the firm can be and the easier it will be to accomplish the transition of ownership, or management, or both.

Not everyone completely agrees. This is surprising, really, since the separation of ownership and management authority is so prevalent in transitions within family-owned firms generally. A founding generation very commonly confers ownership on all members of the succeeding generation of the family, but only those members with actual familiarity with the business and appropriate talent are given any management authority. The managing family member does so for the benefit of all the family member owners; but those nonmanagers are usually heavily constrained from exerting any interference in the conduct of the business.

Perhaps this expectation of a separation of equity and management is not more readily apparent because "family" transitions are so rare in the professional services fields. Unlike many other kinds of businesses, here it's usually not enough to just be a son or daughter; one must usually also have the professional credentials as an accountant, lawyer, architect, or financial planner to be a serious contender for the role of the new boss.

The case of Lyle and Chris Benson, father and son professionals in their tax accounting and financial planning firm, L K Benson & Co., proves this point. Lyle believes that he's solved his firm's transition issues by finding, in his son, a very talented, eager, and credentialed successor. However, he noted at the end of his interview that he has two other children not involved in the business. "I have to figure out how to deal fairly with them." This is exactly the challenge that many other family businesses face. Distinguishing the ownership of the firm from its management will probably lead in the direction of a solution.

Despite this common family business framework, many industry participants and commentators just assume that management and equity always go hand in hand. Phrases like "earning a seat at the table" or "having a stake in the firm's success" or "having skin in the game" often imply that having an ownership interest in the firm, however small, gives that owner some voice in the decision making about the firm's business. Or, in the other direction, the implication is that the firm's management is conducted only by those having ownership stakes.

However, dealing only with implications—not being clear about who gets to decide what and when and how—can create enormous problems of frustrated expectations on all sides. So, at least, being explicit about how congruence of management and ownership play out in the firm is crucial. Usually, of course, at a firm's founding these two elements are unified, often in a very small group or even just one person. As the firm matures, it can—and, we believe, should—separate the two. Not only does this permit the firm to grow faster and better, but it greatly facilitates transitions in both realms.

Aspiriant provides an excellent example, at both the front end and the back. The two predecessor firms (Kochis Fitz and Quintile) started broadly distributing firm equity through direct ownership or phantom stock plans years before their merger in 2008. As of this writing, the firm has more than 50 owners. Meanwhile, they narrowed the governance and management structure into a tightly organized management committee, which reports to the CEO, who in turn reports to a small board of directors, elected from time to time by the owners. Many "own"; very few "manage." When Tim stepped down from his role as CEO, he retained an ownership stake but carried over no management responsibility or authority.

So, to further make our case, let's explore the arguments. Are others uncritical—or just plain wrong—in their thinking? We're convinced, but you be the judge.

Value and Control

There's no doubt that, at least in the aggregate, owners get to call the shots. However, some people stop at this essential notion and don't explore the many nuances that it involves. Whether it's a business owned entirely within a family or, like most professional services firms, owned by people with no genetic relationship to each other, having ultimate control over the business doesn't mean that every owner must participate in every decision all of the time. Some firms that have in fact begun to distribute ownership interests beyond the initial founder(s) still operate in this fashion, having very frequent meetings to discuss and—maybe—decide virtually every question, with every owner having a seat and a voice at the table. Lack of unanimity often stymies timely decisions, and even majority rule often leaves the minority frustrated, since a further argument or more time just might have allowed the decision to go the other way. And where one or just a few owners have most of the voting weight in any event, minority owners can feel that their vote is a sham.

So the reality of ultimate owner control can achieve practical, day-to-day application by limiting the scope of what requires the vote of the owners. Maybe it's major strategic decisions like whether the firm should acquire—or be acquired; maybe it's whether the firm's mission needs to be redefined; maybe it's whether additional owners should be admitted. And maybe there are some issues that are defined as requiring voting by ownership weight; maybe others can be settled by per capita votes. There is no magic formula here. The point merely is that it's not everybody, about everything, all the time. You get to decide how this should be organized for your firm—and you *should* decide!

Even without being deliberate about this, of course, normal human behavior falls into patterns of differentiated decision responsibility. Some people tend to take the reins in certain areas and others acquiesce. But being deliberate about this and having clarity are key in order to avoid frustration and surprise. Yesterday's unconscious pattern can easily become a real problem for someone today—and for someone else tomorrow.

Ultimately, the owners, in the aggregate, usually do have the power—and, we believe, the affirmative and fully conscious duty—to decide who will have the responsibility of managing the firm's day-to-day activities. Who will be endowed with the responsibility to decide all those many other issues that don't rise to the level that require the owners' attention and resolution? That person or those persons need to be selected for their ability, and willingness, to do the job and should be separately compensated (beyond any share of net profits they may be entitled to) for the responsibility they take on. It is very important that they be held accountable for how well they perform against that responsibility and be removable from that job if they don't perform well.

Distribution of Value as a First Step

Probably the most obvious and least controversial feature is that owning a share in the business confers rights to participate in its profits and any proceeds of sale. Many people choose careers in hopes of earning the right to share in these values, and purchasers, of course, do so in order to participate in the expected growth of successful businesses. Consequently, most of the cultural attraction of ownership distribution and most of the commentary around ownership transition involve this notion of financial incentive: the opportunity for buyers to build wealth and, for sellers, the opportunity to liquefy wealth. At the right price, everybody wins!

But we don't think it's optimal to stop the strategic thinking at that point. Let's face it, while people are motivated by money, that's almost never the whole story. Frankly, our view is that the willingness of founders to relinquish ownership is much greater than their willingness to relinquish control over the business. A recent (2014) Pricewaterhouse-Coopers study calls this the "sticky baton" syndrome. Even if ownership is formally transitioned, founders often try to hold on to various elements of control. Here, the separation of management from equity becomes especially important. Because it might be in the best interests of the business for that control to be retained, equity (value) can be distributed without having to distribute the power. Where it is appropriate to do so, the firm's ongoing management can remain in presumably capable hands, with those capable hands earning compensation for that job to boot! Existing founder/CEOs don't have to fear that bringing on new, additional owners necessarily and immediately strips them of their ability to set and implement the firm's direction.

This transition of ownership value is almost certainly an important initial step in transitioning the management power as well, but you have to start somewhere and the entire process can be very gradual. The more this equity transition takes hold and the earlier it starts, the easier the full transition—of power and value—becomes.

The Founder's Financial Dilemma

Having said all of this, a struggle unavoidably arises for founders and successors. Regardless of how much founders and successors love their clients and wish only the best outcomes for their businesses, money has to enter into the equation. Rudy Adolf, CEO of Focus Financial Partners, describes three common dilemmas founders face. After investigating hundreds of firms and making a number of deals, he summarized the ways many firms ultimately transition and the suboptimal impacts those paths have for both the successor(s) and the founder(s):

1. **Downing the plane:** The founder milks the business. It either runs into the ground or the founder tries to sell when the plane is already too low to the ground. There are no buyers for that type of business. The founder might sustain lifestyle and sometimes even achieve larger financial goals through this strategy, but clients and successors almost certainly lose.

2. **Founder as hostage:** The founder allows the successors to become too strong. These successors put the founder in a corner and a deal gets accomplished at an excessive discount (much more on discounts in Chapter 7). The successors likely win here and the founder likely loses, depending on how ugly this scenario gets.

3. **Bad successor deal:** The founder is able to aggressively monetize by selling into a situation where the successor doesn't want to work or the sale happens at a premium because the founder works the deal too hard. The successor's financial upside is taken away, since the buyer has given that upside to the founder through the premium.

The main reason many firms end up in one of Rudy's three categories is that they wait too long to maximize the balance of financial ramifications for all parties. Remember, doing nothing, for now, is a choice, but it runs the risk of waiting too long. One of the reasons firms wait is because they continue to "run numbers" over and over, trying to determine the value of the firm to either an outside or an inside party. One key admonition of all the investment bankers we talked to is to not overthink and continually run the numbers! If you decide you want to really do an outside transaction, the good acquirers are already going to have their models and well-developed analysis of your valuation. It's best to let them go first and then react to what they bring to the table. They are not going to be swayed in the beginning by your world-class analysis, using your variables. And, when it's an internal equity succession, it's best to get a third party to value the firm anyway to minimize (but still not eliminate) emotions around the financial terms of the transaction.

The Successor's Financial Dilemma

Successors face a dilemma equally as concerning. In many current deal structures, the successor works hard only to make the business more expensive for them to buy. Let's say a cadre of next-generation owners will be the equity successors at a firm. They finalize an agreement with the founder, stipulating that they will buy 25 percent of the firm today based on a valuation of 2.5 times revenue, another 25 percent three years from now, and more following that. These successors work hard in the business every day to grow it. However, for every $1 they bring into the firm in new revenue, it costs them $2.5. At first glance that doesn't appear to incent those successors to work very hard. This is an overly simple look at the problem because it ignores the long-term durability of that $1 of revenue and whether its net earnings provide a fair return on the $2.5 purchase price. With a 30 percent net margin, for example, that 30 cents of incremental profits, every year, could present a very handsome 12 percent return, if that revenue and that margin are in fact durable. $2.5 could be a horrendous rip-off or a tremendous bargain. The point, again, is that third-party valuations provide a strong dose of reality and can quell successors' potential for emotional overresponse. Still, the risk of deep dissatisfaction is there. This is where the discipline of expert, third-party valuations can really prove their worth. Both successors and founders need external reality checks.

Almost regardless of the price, most younger equity successors don't have sufficient liquid resources to make the deal work. Without a great deal of support, going to banks is generally a nonstarter. Their balance sheets are very thin: maybe a 401(k) retirement account and a house already under a mortgage. The ability of many successors to generate adequate purchasing power, without a seller-financed note or some creative outside source, is almost nonexistent. We address those options in Chapters 6 and 7.

Building for an Exit Doesn't Maximize Value

Assuming as gospel the valuation metrics and attractive examples one hears or reads about can not only cause an inflated belief in the firm's value but create a flawed belief that certain short-term tactics increase a firm's value, for a sale, when in fact those tactics can actually decrease its value. Let's look at just one simple, but fairly common, example of this flawed thinking.

Let's say a founder goes to an industry conference and attends a presentation that determines their business is worth "six times free cash flow." Some founders will believe that this valuation metric is absolute, set in stone, unmindful of the multitude of specific circumstances and strategic business plan choices (and the quality of their execution) that have yielded that generalization. Consequently, they can fall into the trap of arbitrarily cutting current expenses or of failing to invest in the future of the business to maximize that free cash flow. Very often this means failing to adequately invest in the future of the successor. Such founders could argue that whatever they were paying the successor was decreasing the value of the business by six times that compensation package. In reality, of course, the multiple someone is willing to pay is based on many factors, including the strength of the successor environment. Having a successful team in place to manage the business after the founder exits is generally a prerequisite for getting any reasonable offer to purchase the business.

Charles Goldman and Mark Hurley, CEO of Fiduciary Network, are consistent in their view on this topic. They believe that too many businesses start looking at transition and immediately begin thinking about an exit. This can cause the focus on the business itself to waver. Goldman urges leaders to "build the best firm you can, first. The best way to maximize value is to have a great firm. Great firms have great people, are growing, and focus on the client first. Regardless of the transition strategy a business adopts (sale, internal succession, merger, acquisition, etc.) the best businesses give themselves a great hand to play in all scenarios."

Hope Is Not a Strategy

The transition process often starts with the choice of many potential pathways, but getting anywhere near the desired value for the firm eventually requires committing to one. Rob Francais believes many owners prefer to go down a path to the future involving an internal succession, but, as a fallback position, run the business under the Rudy Adolf description of "downing the plane," merely hoping a buyer will come in out of nowhere and buy the firm. This lack of focus allows them to make poor strategic decisions, which ironically keeps suitors from showing up at all.

Some of the top advisory businesses in the country have achieved their status because they are committed to a strategy. Jeff Thomasson believes that they are successful at Oxford precisely because they don't think about selling. They have taken that option completely off the table. They don't wonder about whether someone might drive a truckload of cash into their boardroom. They don't think about what it would be like to have some even larger organization buy their business. They are committed to one thing: continuing to build and continuing to transition to future generations of leaders what they believe is the best client service organization in the country.

The Great Risk Divide

In 2003, Nik Wallenda completed a death-defying stunt, broadcast live on worldwide television. He crossed a section of the Grand Canyon on a 2 inch wide cable spanning 1,400 feet … 1,500 feet above the ground! Not only did he battle 30-mile-per-hour winds, he also made the walk wearing no harness or safety gear of any kind. It was a sight to behold. It was impossible not to be in awe of the vast Grand Canyon backdrop to Wallenda's feat. It was also hard to ignore how crazy it seemed to attempt it. To many, the transition process feels like this stunt.

We hope that the first section of this book helped make it obvious that successors and founders need to arrive on common ground for the vision of the future of the firm. Your response to this might have been, "Of course!" Still, many people miss one of the foundational issues of why that is so important. It isn't only so the company operates effectively, has the right culture, and the right people, performing the right client service. These are vitally important, but having that common vision also helps to stave off the conflicts that can arise from the often differing risk profiles of the founder and successor.

There may be a great risk divide—a Grand Canyon of sorts—in the financial transactions during transition. This difference in perspective on risk can make it very difficult for founder and successor to fully understand their different perspectives on other issues, mitigate the actual risks, and successfully cross the tightrope.

People often go right to a battle over valuation—but the numbers are the numbers. As Mark Hurley puts it, "The markets in the financial wealth management and investment management industries are extremely efficient because almost all buyers are accessing capital from the same markets. Thus the valuations (what someone is willing to pay) end up almost exactly the same." The difference for the parties to the transaction is in their perceived risk-adjusted returns from those numbers. They don't struggle so much with the calculation; they struggle to accept the outcomes of that calculation. Each side tends to view the risks associated with the transaction very differently.

Most advisory businesses were founded with little capital up front. The founder's financial risk was being able to continue to make mortgage payments and keeping a reasonable lifestyle despite little current income at the outset. The risk seemed great, but in hindsight it was pretty readily tolerated. Most founders were (are!) entrepreneurs, predisposed to taking risk. They were willing to jump out of a plane and put the parachute together on the way down. They were willing to bet on themselves. In advisory businesses, it took only small amounts of capital to make that bet. Now, as these firms have grown, their valuations have grown at an ever faster pace. For successors to bet on themselves now, the amount of capital needed is significantly greater.

We've heard some founders call the successor generation "wimps" for not being willing to take out debt to "bet on themselves." In some cases that's true. In most cases it's not. There can be a large disconnect between the past risks taken by founders and the future risks that successors face. Bernie Clark suggests that successors remember they are buying stable cash flow. "The reason successors should be willing to pay so much for these businesses is that they are buying stable cash flow. When the founders first created their firms, they didn't have any cash flow to buy. Successors shouldn't forget this fact." Fair point made by one of the industry's leading executives.

However, the key word in Bernie's comments is "stable." The successor may need to understand and have confidence in that stability to justify leveraging his or her house to buy a piece of a firm, no matter how the actual valuation numbers work out. This can be very scary, maybe even a more troubling experience than many founders went through as they forewent income for perhaps many months as they started the business. The real issue may be not so much the threats to success but the amount of money actually at stake. For most founders, it was probably not very much really; for many successors today, the numbers can be staggering.

Moreover, the definition of stability relies on the successors' view of their role in controlling the future of the business. Where are they in taking over responsibility for the client relationships? In influencing the overall direction of the firm? In authority to make important operational decisions? Eric points out that "many founders have turned over very little management control or responsibility for the client relationships. I tend to view my advice to other successors through the same lens I use in giving advice to clients. If my client came to me and said they were going to leverage themselves to buy a piece of a privately held business, with little understanding of their control over the future of the business or the client relationships which determine the value of the business, I could never recommend they take out debt to buy that asset."

This is at the heart of the interplay between the operational and the financial discussions founders and successors are already beginning to have—and will need to have, even more, in the years ahead. The issues of management control and client control need to be settled before the transition's financial discussions can make serious progress. So, while broadening of equity ownership may in fact come first, it can't happen without some clarity about how management control will eventually play out. Many firms remain dictatorships, with the founder or founder group having virtually absolute control. That situation is impossible for a successor to feel truly comfortable with. Becoming an owner in a business doesn't necessarily confer management control, and maybe it shouldn't, but, at the very least, equity successors must know how that power will be exercised, under what circumstances, and at what times. Without being comfortable with how current income is split, how reinvestment to grow the firm will work, and how minority owners are protected, few are going to be eager to make a financial deal. In Chapter 6 we show how firms can effectively take on this challenge.

KEY TAKEAWAYS:

1. Firms that don't widen ownership have little chance of a successful transition, without the purchase of the firm by an outside party.
2. Founders hoarding ownership are building an employee-based model at their firms. Ironically, this is the type of environment that initially inspired those same founders to leave their previous employment to start their own firms.
3. Founders and successors each face financial dilemmas. Compromise has to happen for each to meet their own personal goals.
4. Founders have to commit to a strategy. Starting down an internal transition path, only to keep an eye out for an external buyer, leads to a lack of clarity and operational success.
5. The greatest problem in the financial transactions of transition is the great divide between founders and successors in how and where they view risk: the risk taken to start the firm (founders) and the risk presented in the future operations of the firm (successors).

Chapter 6

Splitting the Pies: Defining What Is Enough

Most folks are as happy as they make up their minds to be.
—*Abraham Lincoln*

Absent a clear understanding of what specific financial goals one is trying to achieve, one can just continue to chase more and more money, never knowing what the finish line should be. Many founders have made their dreams come true—at least those they might have articulated years ago. Not following the advice they give their clients, many don't periodically reevaluate how their desires and their wherewithal actually stack-up. They've started and grown successful firms, they've given careers to many people, and now they sit with an opportunity to monetize the value that has been created, through an internal equity succession or an external transaction. That opportunity for "enough" is easy to miss. Failing to genuinely assess what is, in fact, enough can lead to always wanting more. Randy Webb, CEO of Signature, uses a great analogy: "Everything has a goal or a limit. Businesses and financial wealth are like trees. They can grow, but they eventually have some limit. Trees can't grow into space."

Consider the extraordinary wealth of Warren Buffett. In 2014, according to Forbes's list of the world's richest people, he was worth $73 billion, but he was not the richest person in the world. There can be only one person with the most money: his friend and sometimes bridge partner, Bill Gates. So Warren is either already satisfied with his capability to do everything he truly wants and is now just pursuing the fun of it—or he's still chasing the number one slot. Our guess is the former, not the latter. On a much smaller scale, of course, when owners and successors don't have a real, and current, understanding of what they are trying to achieve, discontent and misunderstandings can easily occur. That struggle almost always arises in the discussion of what a firm is worth.

Only One Thing Really Matters

Jay remembers the first time he learned about what something is truly worth. He was 10 years old. As a Cincinnati kid, he was a huge baseball fan of the Cincinnati Reds. At the time, Barry Larkin, now a Hall of Fame shortstop, was fairly new on the scene. From time to time when Jay and his mother would go to the store, she would let him use his allowance to buy a set of Topps baseball cards. Baseball card collectors out there will remember that you really just wanted the gum first and foremost. You loved the stick of gum in the package, even though enjoying it could end up with a trip to the dentist. But you also dreamed of opening a pack of cards and finding a rookie card. Rookie cards (from a player's first full season in the major leagues) were always more valuable. If you were lucky enough to get a rookie card for a big-name player, you were set. One day Jay opened a card package and he felt like he had just gotten a golden ticket as he unwrapped a Barry Larkin rookie card.

There was no Internet then, but there were reference books that listed each card and its value based on the condition the card was in. Jay's pristine Barry Larkin card was listed at $15. In 1989, to a 10-year-old kid, $15 seemed like a lot of money. Jay's dad took him to the store, knowing full well his son wasn't getting $15 for the card. But Jay had high hopes. The store owner looked at the card, agreed with Jay that the card was in great condition, and proceeded to offer him $8. "I remember being confused, upset, and astounded all at one time," Jay said. "My dad negotiated the offer up to $10, which made me feel a little better, but I still walked out confused. I almost cried. How could that guy take $5 from me? My dad bent down to my eye level and said, 'You just learned something you should never forget. Something is only worth what someone is willing to pay for it. It doesn't matter if the magazine said it was $15 if that guy is the only buyer and he's only willing to pay you $10.'" And therein lies the lesson.

Jay learned it when he was 10. A thing is worth only what someone is willing to pay for it. We all know this to be true, but in transitioning businesses, owners sometimes forget. Whether you work at or own a law firm, investment firm, accounting firm, or another advisory business, you and your employees attend conferences, where, in one of the more well-attended breakout sessions, an investment banker or consultant talks about valuation of your business. In accounting firms or law firms, it may be 1 to 1.25 times revenue or 3 to 3.5 times free cash flow; in wealth management firms it may be 2.5 times revenue or 5 or 6 times free cash flow. Whatever number this person says is taken by many in the audience as a solid, baseline frame of reference—call it a "conference contagion" that many people fall prey to. Generally, these speakers are individuals who get paid to get deals done. This means they are usually talking about valuations on the last, highest deal completed. These numbers leave those in the audience feeling pretty good about the valuation of their firm; the math used at the conference becomes "gospel." These presenters aren't trying to mislead the audience. They likely are just trying to educate. However, we all tend to view information through our own filters, and most owners gladly tune their filters toward the higher valuation calculations.

As a result, the valuation in the owner's mind can be significantly inflated beyond a price that buyers will realistically tolerate. It's hard to find a cure for the infection of their inflated belief. This can be very tough on everyone involved. What are a successor and a founder to do? We propose an exercise we believe will help in these difficult financial discussions. But, first, let's explore some big questions that founders and successors must grapple with.

Four Big Questions

Four key questions can help bring clarity to decisions in an equity transition. Their answers are not mutually exclusive; in fact, their impacts intersect.

1. At what age is the founder willing to give up ownership?
2. Does the successor think that time frame is too fast or too slow?
3. Will the firm allow someone, not in a current operating role in the company, to maintain equity ownership?
4. Will the firm require a mandatory retirement date or age triggers when equity must transition?

Defining an Exit Date

One of the common themes of this book is that doing nothing is a choice, though often not a good one. Another key theme is to start early. The first step in trying to start early is to think about a date for equity transition. Most founders tie this to a particular age, believing that that age will correspond to an anticipated accumulation of resources adequate to meet their financial goals. The ability to transition equity is much easier when there is a target age or date. For Joe Sheehan and Eric Kittner at Moneta, determining the exit date for Joe was a give-and-take. However, they both agreed the exercise came to a conclusion when Joe finally told Eric, "My goal is to have no ownership of the practice by the time I'm 70." Once Joe was that clear, they were able to work backward to effectively plan the equity transition.

As an owner, how do you decide this? Get a good financial planner—especially if you are one yourself! Define your financial goals, not only in amount, but in timing, and in relative priority. Especially in talking with firms who dispense financial advice for a living, we've been amazed by the overwhelming lack of financial clarity so many of their owners have about their own circumstances. In many cases the successor becomes the founder's financial advisor, by default, in trying to help the founder get to the "right" answer. This introduces just one more risk, as it's yet another opportunity for conflict to arise. It really isn't fair to either party, but it is extremely unfair for the successor to be put in this position.

Imagine a founder, who relies on a successor or some other employee to design the budget for the business and manage the financials, comes to that successor and asks for help building the founder's retirement model but with no clear-cut ownership exit time frame. There really is no clear way for the successor to win in this situation. The fact that the successor has to suggest a date means likely upsetting the founder no matter what date is chosen.

Successor Concurrence

Ultimately, the successor(s) must agree about that target age or date. Many consultants and conference speakers seem to miss this key point. The founder's perspective dominates; the successor is almost forgotten. Maybe this is not surprising, since it's the founder—or the founder's firm—that is paying for the engagement.

However, the equity exit date has profound implications for the successor. When does the successor feel comfortable taking on broader ownership? When does the successor believe he or she has earned the right to a level of control stemming from that ownership? Does the successor want majority control of the business? Will the successor have to recruit other owners (a few? many?) to assist in the transition, based on the exit date? This is a financial journey not only for the owner but for the successor as well. Here's one area where sensitivity to the successor's timing can gain the founder great improvement in the working relationship with that successor.

Non–Operator Owners

At many firms, maybe especially smaller ones, accepting a *non-operating* owner, either the former founder(s) continuing to own parts of the business, or some new, outside owner(s), may be the only way a transition can occur. Don't let the implementation of the plan get in the way of your thinking about an optimal transition strategy. Acquiring another firm or merger into another firm can help to resolve the equity succession issue, even though that can dramatically change who the operators are.

This is an important cultural question for the future of the business. Mark Tibergien points out why: "Advisory businesses are meant to be owned by those actually currently working in the business. It aligns the owners to the day-to-day needs of those actually working, and very importantly, to the needs of the end client. It's hard to avoid bitter feelings when founders maintain a large piece of the business, but then go to the beach. The successors feel like they are working day to day in the business on a bad financial deal. Regardless of whether this 'bad deal' is true or not, those feelings almost always appear."

Mandatory Sales/Retirement

One way or another, by plan, by force, or just by default, it's "up or out." Almost all companies are built like pyramids. This is not just some coincidence. It's a function of fundamental economics and serves the greater societal good of promoting optimal use of resources. You move up the pyramid (corresponding to greater skill, experience, productivity, and their commensurate rewards) or you move out. But that need only apply to performance on the job(s) involved. It need not, but should, also apply to matters of ownership.

The question remains: How hard does the organization force the movement of ownership from the top of the pyramid downstream? It can always happen much sooner, of course, but you can impose an outer limit. Three firms we have mentioned throughout this book have some sort of mandatory "retirement," and with this retirement comes the mandatory sale of shares. At Oxford that age is 62. Cassady Schiller & Associates has very specific, stepwise rules around equity transition. At age 55, a partner cannot own more than 20 percent. At age 60, that drops to 10 percent, and at the age of 65, partners can no longer have any ownership. At Aspiriant, there is no required retirement age, but owners are required to sell their stake, in five annual installments, beginning at age 70.

Many variables go into whether these requirements are a good idea. To complete a sale, you need a buyer. To have a forced retirement or sell-by age also requires a successor group to be in place, often with access to a friendly lender or an outside capital source to take the shares off the market. It seems the best way to handle this is to actually have this seller/buyer discussion and actually make rules so that everyone can organize their planned decisions around them. Rules can always be changed if circumstances warrant, but having no rules invites chaos and almost certainly produces frustration on all sides. Having an articulated policy removes one difficult "land mine" in the succession process. As successors, Jay and Eric believe it's a very good thing; it takes pressure off the conversation and brings organizational clarity. Nobody wonders, "When is that partner going to be moving on, and how much will it cost me when he does?"

The Pie-Slicing Exercise

In the Supplemental Materials, there is a framework for determining how to split the cash and equity value of the company. You might think of it as slicing up a pie. There really are four pies that a firm needs to slice. They come in two flavors: cash and equity. (See Figure 6.1.)

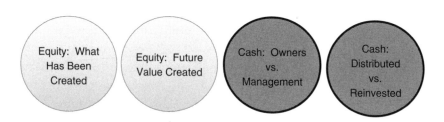

Figure 6.1   Equity and Cash Exchange

Slicing the Equity

What's Been Created: There are two value calculations important to the equity transition of the company. The first one is the value of the firm today. It represents the value for the cumulative effort that has been built. But, realistically, that current value represents what a buyer believes about the firm's future. Tibergien says it bluntly: "Value is a function of the future." Still, how long the successor has already been around and what his or her role was in building the firm will determine whether or not that successor "deserves" any share of what exists today. Brand-new successors should not reasonably expect to be given a piece of a pie they didn't create.

What Will Be Created: The upside of the equity, the future, is a different story. Here, the successors can claim a substantial share. But the proper size of that slice is not clear. The successor might be right to claim a larger part of this pie if he or she is leading the firm to its new future. However, that new value is being produced on a platform of client relationships and service reputation the founder created. The share can't be completely tied just to respective future workloads. A lot of the "work" was done a long time ago, and its value endures.

Slicing Up the Cash

Management versus Ownership

One of the most important aspects of the pie-slicing exercise involves separating payment for ownership from payment for doing a job. As we addressed in Chapter 5, at the founding of firms there was little need for this distinction. Founders owned all or very large portions of the business and made all the business decisions. Management and ownership were unified. The firm's profits and the owner compensation were, on fundamental economics, one and the same. The owner did most of the management work, so the workload and compensation were closely aligned. However, as a founder steps away and may no longer do most of the work of management, it becomes highly demotivating for a successor to have the founder expect the same level of compensation as before.

The common denominator among the firms that have been successful in transitioning is that they solved this problem. It's not easy, but it's critical. As we began to explore in Chapter 5, separating ownership (and its rewards) from management (and its compensation) flies in the face of a lot of conventional wisdom.

As a firm grows and achieves greater success as a business, there are more profits (cash flow) and greater enterprise value (equity) to share. Hoarding that for one owner or within a narrow group of owners can have three interrelated and potentially bad results:

- It can make the price of acquiring ownership too daunting for all but the most highly resourced external buyers.
- It can seduce the current owner(s) into too great a dependency on very large net earnings cash flows.
- It can severely diminish the attractiveness of that business as a career choice for talented and ambitious employees, and that, in turn, can threaten the ongoing value of the firm.

Consequently, the prevailing ethic is to encourage founders or narrow ownership groups to begin the equity distribution process early, to attract the next generations of talent. That starts them early on building their wherewithal to eventually fully liquefy the ownership interests of that founder or narrow group. This implies, of course, that equity interests are in fact rewarded by a share of the net earnings of the firm. Cash flows to the owners, as owners. But before that can happen, cash must first flow to those doing the work of the business in the form of compensation for the jobs they are doing. If the successor is performing an important (maybe the most important) job in the business, the successor needs to be paid for that effort. If that means the successor gets paid both as a key manager and as an owner, we believe that's the way it should be.

Especially here, we find it important to distinguish that "start the equity distribution early" ethic from its impact on the firm's management. Not every owner needs to or should manage, and not every manager needs to be an owner. Not every new owner has the talent or the stomach for management responsibility. As Bob Oros, head of Fidelity's services to the RIA market, puts it: "A real, durable transition requires that owners must be comfortable in reporting to managers. This is essential not only to their own accountability but to management's ability to actually run the business." People can't be permitted to play their ownership card to escape responsibility—to the firm's management—for accomplishing the firm's business objectives. To allow that would let very valuable resources go under-utilized or misdirected and could easily diminish management's authority over other staff as well.

But that management responsibility, then, must be supported by actual competence in the position(s). Appropriate characteristics for management responsibility can be summarized by three A's:

Age: A manager must be old enough to have both internal and external credibility but still young enough to have sufficient time to actually achieve performance over a reasonable period. Relying on someone within just a year or so of his or her own retirement can be a waste of a genuine developmental opportunity.

Aptitude: The talent for management responsibility needs to be present. Not everyone can do this, and some don't really have the raw material for it to be developed.

Appetite: Management is difficult. It can involve important sacrifices in time and effort and in relationships within the firm and at home. If someone needs to be coaxed into the job, he or she is probably not the right candidate.

Further, the scale of the business can change. As the firm grows—say, from 3X clients to 10X and from net earnings of $2Y to $15Y— there are many scale advantages. One of these is in the ranks of management. As a firm achieves client and profit and distributed ownership scale, it does not need to duplicate that scale advance in management. That 10X client/$15Y profit firm still needs only one CEO, one operating chief, one head of the human resources (HR) function, and so on. Hiring the finest talent to fill those managerial and submanagerial roles, and paying them accordingly, does not require that those jobholders necessarily be owners themselves—at least not on the day they're hired.

Clearly, the firm might want its key managers to also have an ownership stake, at least eventually; the prospect of eventual ownership may be a crucial recruiting tool in acquiring the right talent. So having an already robust distribution of ownership makes that recruiting tool credible.

Said another way, the interests of the firm's long-range success may require it to look beyond its *current* ranks to find the best talent for the job. Not having to limit itself to its current owners to fill an important management job opens additional pathways to greater success.

So, Should Financial Rewards Be Equal?

In one of our interviews the person was adamant about one rule at his company: "We don't argue about money. If we start arguing about money we've done one of two things wrong. We either aren't growing the firm quickly enough so everyone feels like their piece of the pie is big enough or we didn't select our partners correctly. If we are arguing about money, we aren't focused on our clients and what's best for them. That's not a culture we are going to accept."

We believe that firms need to deal with this provocative thought: Should all partners make the same amount of cash for their respective roles at the firm? Some firms, like the one cited here, believe this is the case. They believe partners should hold each other accountable for business performance, but they also believe that if the partner base is diverse and accountable, each brings an important strength to the business and all roles bring the same benefit to the firm. They believe all partners should receive the same cash for their day-to-day responsibilities, and any differences in amounts should be driven by distributions tied to ownership percentages.

David Cassady believes that the way cash is split isn't really a financial exercise; it's a cultural exercise. His firm comes from the mind-set that all is equal among partners for their day-to-day responsibilities. "I believe our view on this item is different than probably 90 percent of the firms out there and many will disagree with us," he contends. "However, to us it's not about the money. It's about how this belief drives our culture. Our partners are all important to our business. Just because I was one of the founders doesn't mean I'm more important day to day than the partner sitting next to me. He or she is equally important to how we serve our clients and that's why we are in the business in the first place."

With due respect for these points of view, we simply can't agree. There are different jobs in any business, and those jobs have discernible market values in the geographic and talent markets in which any firm operates. Most people would agree that the head of HR, for example, while very important, is not as valuable to the organization as its operating chief or certainly as its CEO. The incumbents for these jobs have alternative employment options. To replace their management talents from the outside would require paying going compensation rates. So differential, market-based pay both serves to have the business conform to the economic realities of the competitive market for talent and greatly helps to eliminate many arguments. It's not so much about the founder and the successor battling over cash as it is about recognizing the imperatives of the competitive market for labor. The "facts" of this are knowable; compensation data is readily available for most jobs in most markets.

Once the compensation-for-labor issue is settled, the still-large (one hopes) profit residual is available to divide on a pro rata ownership basis. Thus, the profit share rewards for ownership (if managers also happen to be owners) are a separate matter. But, first, we believe you also must pay, separately and deliberately, for the talent and the job performance that talent produces. And that's almost never equal.

The Great Reinvestment Debate

The fourth pie relates to the issue of current distributions of available cash or reinvestment of that cash in the future of the firm.

It happens in churches and country clubs all across the United States. A new building, capital investment, or large strategic project is discussed by the leadership team and brought to the membership for discussion and a vote on whether the project should be undertaken. The cost of the project will be spread across the membership, with everyone paying the same amount. The younger members, for the most part, love the projects because they see a long future era for reaping the returns on this investment, while many older members find it difficult to stomach. Their horizon of benefit is much shorter. Whose money is being spent, and who is getting the greatest return on that investment? This isn't happening only at churches and country clubs, of course; it happens at all firms in transition.

This can have a much simpler resolution than many people fear. If the pies are sliced appropriately in the prior components of this exercise, this question can readily work itself out. Whoever is getting more of the upside potential should reinvest the most. And if the compensation system has the net earnings of the firm being distributed according to ownership share, that contribution to reinvestment will happen automatically. Any dollar reinvested in equipment, or marketing efforts, or salaries for new hires, and so on, must reduce the amount of the otherwise net income. Larger shareholders automatically pay a larger portion of that investment. However, we see founders who want to maintain a large percentage of the equity upside as well as the current cash flow and still limit the amount they are willing to reinvest in the business. How does this equation make sense? In our view, it doesn't.

Avoid the Path to Neutral

The results of the pie-slicing exercise should produce direct and indirect incentives for both founder and successor. Financial incentives come in all forms and arrangements. The common traits of an effective incentive package incent everyone to make the pie bigger. As the value of the firm grows, even if the existing owners have shrinking percentage stakes, their overall personal net worth climbs, and the new owners enjoy the growth in the value of what they have acquired.

Regardless of the vehicle a firm uses (purchased shares, restricted stock, phantom stock, options, etc.), most successors have equity-oriented deals requiring them to stay for a period of time and/or requiring them to grow the company for that equity to actually deliver incremental value. Any good successor wouldn't want a handout but should be willing to earn growth in equity through helping to produce durable increases in the value of the firm. Regardless of how a firm creates these incentives, everyone wins only if the equity value grows; this means the firm has to grow.

Behavior is driven by incentives. Those incentives don't always have to be just money. Various perquisites or status features (a bigger office, perhaps) can also come into play. In any case, you need to align incentives to maximize, as much as possible, the value of the firm, while fostering the happiness of the person you are incenting. While money isn't everything, it's also not nothing. For example, look at the performance of professional athletes in contract years. Almost without exception, professional athletes outperform their career averages by wide margins in the final years of their contracts and significantly underperform their career averages in the first year following the signing of a new contract. The correlation might be completely innocent, just coincidental. We think not.

In a highly developed overall compensation system, salaries are tied to market values for the job being performed, and incentives (short-term or long-term) are tied to the accomplishment of specific goals (sales, internal training, improvements in operating margins—there is no end to the potential list). Those payments for labor, whether the labor of staff or the labor of the owners, are accounted for in arriving at the net earnings of the firm. Those net earnings are then payable to the owners as the return on their equity. At the outset of most firms, when they are small, have few staff, and are struggling to capture client revenue just to stay in business, this level of sophistication is almost never implemented. It's also not yet really necessary. But as firms grow from being small "practices" to being able to build themselves into durable businesses, the more the compensation arrangement looks like these three elements of salary, bonus, and net earnings share, the more successful the firm is likely to be and the easier it will be to effect transitions of both management and equity.

Further, the first two components impose a discipline on the third, and vice versa. Insisting on an acceptable minimum level of return to ownership will impose a limit on what can be paid in compensation for labor. Payment for those labor components will raise the question of who should also get to share in the profits. If two people are being paid according to their market value and being rewarded with bonuses for their special performance, but only one of them is an owner, the nonowner will ask, "Why not me, too?" There are many answers (tenure, poise, initiative, and many more that can't really be captured in competitive market values), but you'd better have some kind of answer.

There is a risk in creating any incentives. You will get what you pay for. Make sure it's what you want. So founders need to look at incentives from a good successor's point of view. Once you incent a high-performing successor, you better want to take the company where the incentives are motivating him or her to take it. This sounds obvious, but it's often ignored in the daily operation of a business. As we reviewed in Section I, the owners of firms really need to answer the tough question "Do you want to grow?" When reading Section I you may have wondered why this question even mattered or if it mattered whether you answered the question honestly. This is why it matters.

Regardless of the size of your firm or where you are in the evolution of your firm, eventually your growth will plateau if you don't challenge the status quo. Growth takes investment; it takes pushing the envelope, maybe completely redesigning the firm from what it looks like today into a better future. This is often one of the big benefits of transition; maybe only the successor can see that better future. For their own financial well-being, successors not only want to push the envelope but also probably need to do so.

Defining What's Enough—a Real Case

Eric knows firsthand how difficult it is to help founders determine what's enough and to get clear on their financial goals. When the time came for him to talk with John Henry about the financial aspects of a transition, the room got really quiet. Hearing "Now, is the time to start selling shares or reducing compensation" probably isn't very welcome. Eric had to put his problem-solving skills to work, overtime.

Eric started thinking through the levers that were available to push or pull over the course of the transition to help protect John Henry's lifestyle but also allow for an eventual "pot of gold" at the end of the rainbow. Having an objective compensation philosophy and structure that forms the basis of pay for all employees, including the owners, was a key foundation. With that in place, the foundation was set to solve the real problems.

Let's look, conceptually, at the financial life cycle from a founder's perspective and from a successor's perspective. Founders often view ownership rewards starting at basically zero but then growing until a point at which the firm begins to achieve significant economies of scale, especially in very well run firms. From that point, those rewards track with the firm's growth and profitability. Simultaneously, however, the founder's compensation for labor need not. It is more reflective of market comparables for the position and actual performance on the job.

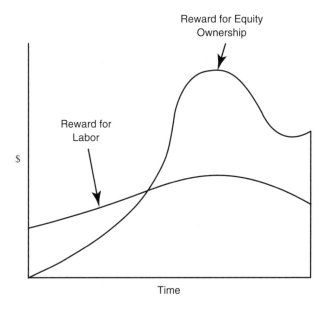

Figure 6.2 Founder's Financial Life Cycle

The financial reward for ownership can eventually substantially exceed the financial reward for labor, as shown in Figure 6.2. This is a worthy goal and not an uncommon occurrence in professional service firms.

Successors can enter this picture at almost any point. If the successors begin to acquire some equity interest, in addition to their compensation for their labor, they are likely to cause the founder's reward for equity to expand over time. Even though the founder's share of the profits may initially decline with the share of ownership acquired by successors, the eventual absolute size of the profit share can increase as the successors grow the business to make their equity acquisition worthwhile.

In addition, of course, the founder is receiving consideration of some kind for the equity share he or she is selling. Correspondingly, the successors are paying that consideration. The overall net economics for the successors can be very modest, or even negative, for a while, in expectation of very substantial rewards in the future. The overall net economics for the founder can be very substantial during that early phase, declining gradually and eventually to zero once retired from any employment and all ownership has been sold.

This was how Eric resolved the seven-year transition of his founder, so that John Henry's spendable cash flow actually grew, even while his labor compensation declined—ultimately to zero—and his ownership was being sold gradually to the next generation. This was because the firm doubled in value over that seven-year period. The Austin Asset successors also believed they needed to reward John Henry for their use of the platform he and Eric had built. John Henry is able to reap the benefits of the firm's continued growth as he gets yet a further bite at the apple in the future, by granting him a form of option on the growth in value of the firm four years after his final sale.

What a Successor Should Ask For

Internal successions only get accomplished when there is an abundance of fairness. Emotions run high and can cause all parties to define fairness differently. These emotion-laden elements are the focus of the final section of this book. For now, as we think about this from a successor's point of view, we see the financial and governance aspects intertwined. We believe there are things a successor needs to feel comfortable with in the deal. The point here is not to put specific percentages, or numbers, or optimal structures to these considerations, as all cases are unique. The point is that these are the items to be negotiated to some satisfactory result:

1. **Agreements on cash flow:** Whether by actual contract or by other reliable or self-enforcing arrangements, dividends to be received from ownership and current income/compensation for management roles should be clear and enforceable. The successor cannot be expected to assume the added risk of having his or her overall cash flow impacted by arbitrary decisions. If, like Captain Renault in the film *Casablanca,* you are "shocked!" that someone could be arbitrary, think again. Negotiate some reasonable guarantees.

2. **Outside valuation:** An expert, outside party should appraise the value of the firm. That appraisal should be reevaluated from time to time. Once every two or three years is a reasonable expectation.

3. **Reinvestment:** Some agreement on how reinvestment in the future of the firm will be shepherded needs to be in place.

This could come in the form of a board committee or an internal management committee. What is important to the ongoing success of the business must come first and be separated from decisions about personal compensation.

4. **Minority ownership protection:** If the successor is taking on a minority ownership stake, the governance model should have something in place to protect them from potential abuse by the majority.

5. **Reliance on their own advisors:** It's common in small firms for a successor and founder to be potentially represented by the same legal counsel or financial advisor. This may make sense and can help keep transaction costs down, but the successor shouldn't overly rely on parties who may not be able to be completely impartial. So, no matter how cordial the discussions are, it's probably a good idea for the successor to retain outside tax, legal, and planning advice, independent of all parties at the firm. What's more, the successor should request payment support from the firm for this advice. Most likely the founder is running the cost of his or her advisors through the business. It is a legitimate expense for the business; the same is true for the successor.

Now that the firm has determined the ways it wants to slice the pie, it's time to think about making a deal.

KEY TAKEAWAYS:

1. Founders and successors cannot afford to calculate value based on blanket valuation metrics they hear about at conferences or read about in trade publications. Use an expert, third-party appraisal based on the details of your specific business.

2. Slicing the cash and equity pies is difficult, but going through the exercise step by step tends to minimize misunderstanding or animosity.

3. Separating compensation for labor from profit share rewards for ownership will solve many problems in achieving solutions to

business organizational problems. It's almost certain to greatly facilitate the transitions of management responsibility and equity ownership.

4. Founders can and should come to an understanding of "how much is enough."

5. Successors are right to mitigate their risks by negotiating reliable assurances.

Chapter 7

Let's Make a Deal

Life consists not in holding good cards, but in playing those you
hold well.

—Josh Billings

We spent much of Chapter 6 trying to define the major building
blocks of transition strategy by working through the personal financial
impacts for both founders and successors. Current owners have four
financial options: (1) retain a predominant ownership stake in the company, risking an eventual drop in equity value (hoping meanwhile to get
enough cash out of it); (2) complete an internal succession by selling
shares at a discount; (3) bring in outside capital to assist in an internal
transition; or (4) sell or merge the business. For a successor, the guiding
principle in any of these scenarios is that, while the founder needs to be
treated fairly, the transition strategy can't be so favorable to the founder
that the successor retains too little upside.

Let's assume for the rest of this chapter that option 1, milking the
business, is off the table. As we've emphasized, "doing nothing"—for

now—is a legitimate strategy. But it can't be a permanent one. At some point, the strategic focus must move toward one of the other options, if it's not too late. Strategic delay can become a form of perennial denial, permitting the founder to cultivate the delusion that there will, someday, be some attractive rescue. No one lives forever. Not overcoming denial will not have a happy ending. When is that optimal time to choose a more affirmative strategy? There is no general answer, but in the preceding chapters we've tried to identify an important clue as being the point at which the urging of successors and the calculated "enough" for founders coincide.

Discounting Is the Name of the Game

Where the affirmative strategy is an internal succession, the almost always essential financial element is a discount to what the "external" value may be. That discount provides the mechanism for the existing owners and the new to share in the value that has been created (mostly, but not entirely, going to the founders) and the value of the future of the business (mostly, but not entirely, going to the successors). The amount of that discount depends on many factors. There is no magic rule. Still, discounts in the neighborhood of 25 to 30 percent are common—greater if the future is especially risky; less if the stability of revenue streams is high and growth trajectories are strong. The expert, third-party appraiser can usually offer an estimate of two values, one where the transaction is to an outside buyer who is acquiring complete control and another, lower, one where internal buyers are purchasing minority interests.

Further, an internal transaction is often facilitated by installment payments and favorable financing. That financing can come directly from the seller or be arranged (and usually guaranteed) by the firm from a conventional third-party lender or other succession facilitator. (More on those third party facilitators later in this chapter.)

The discount reflects the economic reality of closely held businesses, generally. Outside of the realm of publicly traded and publicly priced enterprises, there is too much uncertainty and too much illiquidity to command a "full" external price. Through an agreed-upon discount, buyers and sellers share the illiquidity and the uncertainty. It's about being fair to all parties. But part of that fairness is ensuring that successors don't demand too great a discount and then, soon thereafter, retransact the business to an eager external buyer, capturing the value of that original discount into their own pockets. Wise sellers demand some protection. That could be in the form of any installment payments being "repriced" at the then going value of the firm and/or "tag along" provisions that give former owners some piece of the enhanced valuation of a third-party transaction for some period of time. Realistically, successors in turn demand that the "tag along" deteriorate over time—perhaps it's 100 percent in the first year, two-thirds in the second, one-third in the third, zero after that. Internal transitions need to be governed by a strong notion of fairness on all sides. One's colleagues are continuing to own and run the business. Negotiations probably can't be completely at "arm's length." An expectation of maximizing every last dollar of value, whether by sellers or buyers, will probably doom the attempt to get to an agreement.

In the special, and, for professional services firms, somewhat unusual, case of a succession within the family, the discount may be a deliberate tactic. It can be used both to minimize gift taxes on the values transferred to the next generation and to minimize estate taxes by moving as much as possible of the future growth in the value of the business out of the estate of the founder generation.

Importantly, this notion of discount becomes a permanent proposition so long as the ongoing transition of the business to successive generations of owners remains internal. The discount may decline as the business grows and revenue streams demonstrate great stability over time; it could also widen, of course, if new elements of risk enter the picture. But, in any event, no internal succession will ever occur at full, third-party-buyer prices.

External Capital

For larger firms, some specialty banks will back certain succession transactions. However, this often requires the selling owner(s), to personally guarantee the debt and almost always requires the firm to provide that guarantee as well. Like direct seller-to-buyer financing, many owners find this unappealing because the transaction isn't really complete if they are backstopping the debt, even though they've already had to pay tax on the gains the "sale" produced. Nevertheless, those banks tend to take a very hands-off approach to the operations of the firm, looking only to have the loan be paid back, either by the buyer or by the business or by the personal guarantors. Dustin Mangone, of PPCLOAN, specializing in organizing bank transition financing for professional services firms, observes that "loans are relatively easy for firms with strong earnings that are sufficient to cover debt payments at a debt service coverage of 4 or 5 to 1." For creditworthy borrowers, there are very few strings attached.

Some of the dominant custodians for the wealth management industry, such as Schwab, are willing to provide a level of financing to facilitate transitions. It is in their interest, of course, to assist their customers to remain successful. However, as Liz Nesvold, head of M&A advisory firm Silver Lane Advisors, observes, custodians usually present only a partial answer. Because of the other and more substantive business they do with these firms, they are reluctant to be too large a creditor, not wanting to be the heavy if the debt turns sour.

In a somewhat similar fashion to bank financing, some venture firms are willing to supply capital, not for a direct equity stake but in exchange for some share of the firm's revenue or preferred share of the net earnings. The size of that share and how long it might last is a matter of negotiation. However, other than a requirement that key personnel stay on board for at least some time, there are few strings attached.

At the furthest extreme there are the "aggregators." In the wealth management industry, firms such as Rudy Adolf's Focus Financial and Mark Hurley's Fiduciary Network are available to supply transition capital. But, here, there are some strings, although not necessarily bad ones.

As the category description implies, the approach here is to "aggregate" firms to achieve significant scale, with common support infrastructure and centralized regulatory compliance. Their goals are either an eventual public offering for that aggregated set of firms or some version of commonly shared infrastructure, marketing assistance, and governance sophistication under very long term financing arrangements. They are definitely not "hands-off." These deep-pocketed firms buy minority or even majority stakes in a business and provide strategic support to the management teams. Generally speaking, they have very well honed and flexible deal-making apparatuses and have a clear picture of the kinds of firms they want to bring into their orbit. They tend to come looking for you; you don't really need to apply.

Lessons from Other Professional Services Businesses

By the way, accounting firms and law firms have not seen this push to consolidation from outside aggregators. Instead, mergers or outright acquisitions by similar firms appear to be the current trend in these industries. The major driver of that difference probably relates to the strength of the recurring revenue streams in the respective businesses. Firms with strong recurring revenue and high margins even after compensating the professional talent, like wealth management firms, garner much higher valuations today. That, in turn, makes internal succession almost impossible without some substantial discount to the value for the transaction or the use of outside capital, even after that discount. Other kinds of professional services firms don't tend to have aggregators today because they don't tend to need them. But there may be an important clue to the future here.

It could be that, due to a combination of factors, the economics within advisory/wealth management firms will gradually shift toward more of a "very high compensation while employed, but relatively low capital multiples at transition" model. Like contemporary consulting, architecture, accounting, and law firms (all professional services industries that have already experienced many generations of owner transitions), principals of advisory/wealth management firms over the coming decades may come to enjoy very high levels of compensation during their working years and generous retirement and deferred compensation packages, but only relatively nominal capital accounts. Pricing and service pressure from increasingly robust technological delivery mechanisms, increasing commoditization of investment applications, and the sheer absolute size of the growing values of advisory/wealth management firms may force movement in this direction over the next several generational transitions.

Perhaps the economics of wealth management 30 or 40 years from now will look more like the economics of accounting or law today. That could be a very good thing for society—and for the practitioners at work in those advisory firms of the future—if that economic shift permits firms to have the stability and durability of these other professional endeavors. Nevertheless, this might be a significant burden on successors transitioning into expensive capital ownership in the nearer term if the countervailing force of high current levels of compensation is slow in coming. Exploring this possible future, in detail, is much beyond the scope of this book; however, we see enough vitality in these possibilities that we encourage our readers to take note and we urge much more intense study of this potential future landscape.

Today's Landscape

So, be that future as it may, the realities of valuations today already usually require some significant help to effect transactions, even if at discounted valuations. We come back to a central theme of this book: Owners have a large array of choices. But, if independence—commanding one's own destiny—is truly important, some external capital sources can get in the way.

Those external capital sources come in a variety of flavors; the "aggregators" have different governance requirements for putting money into a firm. Once one of them has shown an interest in your firm, you can at least use that leverage to shop for better deals somewhere else. In fairness, however, firms willing to bring outside money to advisory business transitions are providing a great service to the industry. Many are concerned that there's not nearly enough available capital to support the many thousands of transitions for small to medium-size firms in the wealth management industry in the coming 5 to 10 years. The more efficient the aggregators' processes and the more finely tuned their structures become, and the more success they can demonstrate, the more competition they will spawn, we believe, and, thus, the more capital will become available for attractive firms, even small ones.

The benefits of outside capital, as well as the drawbacks, are worth exploring.

Culture is often the most important intangible of an advisory business. It helps land clients and recruit talent, and often embodies the independence founders desired when they started their firms. A big risk, often overlooked, of taking outside capital is that it will almost certainly change the culture of the business. Outside capital, even from the most hands-off investor, brings new people to the table. Philip Paleveev likens outside capital to inviting a new acquaintance to a dinner party. "It may turn out fine; many guests are perfectly well-behaved and add a lot of positive energy to the gathering. But, there's always the risk of the dinner guest having a few too many glasses of wine and changing the dynamic of the party in a very bad way."

Part of the excitement of having your own firm is control over your own destiny. It's important that founders and successors are aligned on this issue. Some outside sources might be great for the founder but not so much for the successor. Here are several considerations for both successors and founders regarding outside capital:

The Hotel California: Some liken outside capital to the lyric in the Eagles song "Hotel California": "You can check out any time you like, but you can never leave." Once involved, it can be very difficult to remove the new participant in the business.

Control: In many cases, owners are unwilling to engage in an outright sale because of their sense of loss of control. In many deals involving outside capital, even if that capital is not engaged in some element of a formal sale, owners may be giving up important areas of control without taking an equivalent degree of risk off the table.

Trading Equity: In some outside capital deals, you are trading equity in your own business for equity in that outside firm. Some portion of the purchase is likely to be in the direct equity currency of the capital source. The positive prospect, of course, is for that equity to grow much faster than your own.

Growth: That scary question is here again: Are you willing to do the things necessary to grow the firm? Make no mistake about it: The outside capital providers intend to get their returns. If you don't grow, their return will probably come out of your own pocket.

Mark Hurley believes that a firm's valuation is nothing more than the "accumulated goodwill with the clients." This is what an outside party is buying participation in. No matter how good an outside firm is at due diligence, Mark believes that it is impossible for them to adequately, and thoroughly, assess the risks. Fiduciary Network believes the best person to understand the future value of those client relationships is the successor. We agree! The successor(s) should want to take on the right level of risk to gain a large amount of the upside of the firm. So Fiduciary Network puts much of the financial risk of growing the firm on the successor.

Strategic Advantage: Outside capital sources bring more than just money to the table. They bring scale and a variety of platform features to accelerate future growth. Scale can solve a lot of problems successors will face in transition, providing opportunity for greater upside for the successor(s) as well as for any remaining ownership that the founder will retain.

The outside capital option is an especially interesting one for successors who feel they can grow the firm but don't otherwise have the capital to make that happen. It can't be just about cashing out the founder. No outside capital source is likely to buy that proposition. If they are interested at all, they want to make an investment in the firm's future, not just pay for its past.

So, in deals like these, who gets the cash, when, and why? You need to understand what cash you receive and, more important, what gets invested into the operations of the business. The last thing successors want is to be on the hook to grow the firm (for themselves and to provide returns to the capital source) but not have enough investable cash to really make that happen. You need to ensure that an outside capital strategy doesn't become a "milking the business" proposition in a different form.

The "Second Transaction" Risk: Many outside capital deals happen in two transactions. The first one usually happens immediately, with capital coming in to liquidate some or all of the founder's ownership and to more broadly distribute ownership among others. The second transaction typically occurs sometime between three and seven years later when any remaining founder ownership is liquidated. This second transaction can cause a general change in ownership structure and can also cause the outside capital source to then look at an outright sale or merger to maximize its equity value. This second transaction is often where the greatest risk lies for a successor—or, on the positive side, where the successor's upside opportunity really proves itself.

Ensuring Side-by-Side Ownership: Sometimes, preferential equity vehicles may be created in this kind of transaction. The closer the successor(s) can keep their ownership rights on the same terms as those of the founder, the better. You want as many people on your side of the table as possible. In almost all outside capital scenarios, you will not have complete control, so you need to ensure your interests are aligned with those others who benefit most from the success of the firm. If you are running the firm, it's a reasonable expectation.

In most cases, founders as well as successors will face what they perceive as "less than perfect" scenarios. Assuming you aren't going to simply walk away, you may have to become comfortable with taking the best deal you can get. Adam Birenbaum, CEO of Buckingham Asset Management, comments that Buckingham decided Focus Financial Partners was the right way for them to go. They brought in Focus as a strategic and capital partner because Adam realized it was the best way he had found to treat the founders fairly and also provide the right foundation for growth. As he puts it, "Successors think they will get everything they need to optimize the situation they are in. That's not realistic. I didn't have the capital to buy a firm with billions of dollars under management. It would be crazy for me to think I would not need capital partners to make it all work. There's no perfect solution, but we got to the right solution for everyone in our transaction."

It May Be Time to Consider a Sale or Merger

Much of this book focuses on the hope many firms have to be able to remain completely independent and accomplish a successful internal transition. Section I of this book is devoted to efforts toward building the organizational and operational foundation for doing that internal transition. Section III addresses the emotional roller coaster that any transition—but especially an internal one—involves. Still, there may come a point where a sale or a merger makes the most sense. If an internal deal, even with some outside help, can't be accomplished, a founder will ultimately try whatever has a reasonable chance of achieving his or her most important goals. In contrast, many successors are prone to consider it a failure if the entire business is sold to or merged into another entity. But that new arrangement may well present opportunities that realistically weren't available for successors in the existing scenario.

Outright sale, of course, involves some kind of direct payment, often in installments, often tied to continued employment by key principals, and often with targets for financial performance going forward.

Mergers usually rely on continuing participation in business operations and a reconfigured sharing of the equity of the newly merged organization; very often, little if any cash changes hands.

Most mergers, however, are still a form of acquisition of one firm by another. Rarely are they true mergers of financial equals, despite the rhetoric often used to describe them. "Equivalency" can come, however, in the form of the aggregate worth of complementary characteristics, such as client service capabilities, professional talent, geographic market penetration, client diversification, and management capabilities. Thus, most mergers are a very special kind of "sale"—usually not for cash, but for a share of equity in a new entity where the whole is expected to be greater than the sum of its premerger parts.

Nevertheless, there's no escaping some essential valuation calculation. How much of that new, merged entity's equity will the respective owners of the premerger businesses come to own? If the merger indeed brings complementary advantages, that sharing of the new firm's total value should be accretive to owners of both participating firms—but it won't be equal.

So, in either case, sale or merger, the two financial questions are: Will someone want to buy or merge with your business? Will they pay, or allocate equity sharing on, what you think it's worth?

What Drives Value?

Many founders are stuck between determining whether to continue running the business, finding an external buyer, or finding an internal buyer. These are business organizational and emotional decisions, but if a founder is on the fence, truly understanding what drives value is crucial. David DeVoe has been an advisory business thought leader on transitions for well over a decade. He has developed a screen of 40 value drivers for an acquirer's valuation of a firm. In DeVoe's hierarchy, there are three categories of value drivers: growth, cash flow, and risks. And, as to some of those risks: "Is there someone in the business to keep the clients in their seats? Is the management team truly a team? Is there a single point of failure? If the founder is the only one making investment decisions, for example, a firm is probably worth less."

David sees why acquirers struggle to value and buy advisory businesses: "Only about 25 percent of advisory businesses have developed any kind of succession plan. Once it's obvious to a buyer or merger partner that there's no plan in place other than to sell, founders can't expect to get 'full value.' Although we are hearing 'I don't need a succession plan because I'm going to die at my desk' less frequently than we did a few years ago, we still hear something to that effect shockingly often."

Is the Firm Still Just the Founder?

In the early chapters of this book, we discussed the organizational and client service problems of the founder as the "sun." There can be severe financial consequences as well. The easiest way to minimize sale or merger value is to lack broad infrastructure, systematic governance, organized and reproducible client service, and, most important, motivated, capable staff. Systematic processes and technological infrastructure (for reporting, back-office operations, and client relationship management [CRM]) not only force the disaggregation of responsibility and improve the reliability of the results, they also make it more about the "firm" than about the founder. This heightens the value of the firm for any acquirer or merger partner. Post-transaction, some of that infrastructure may change as people, processes, and systems are integrated, but not having an established, robust base to start with diminishes the firm's attractiveness.

Is Your Firm Strategic?

The biggest driver of value is whether or not your firm is considered strategic to an acquirer. Rob Francais isn't in the business of doing "acquisitions." If Aspiriant does a deal, Rob wants it to be a merger of complementary advantages. The firm's foundation was built as just that: a merger of two already large and successful firms finding synergies. This merger joined visions of lasting independence, distributed ownership, enhanced client service, and industry excellence—all of which were already foundational in both Kochis Fitz and Quintile before the firms came together. Those values continue even more emphatically today.

Many existing advisory firm acquirers look for firms very similar to their own. "Many firms look to acquire firms just like theirs. They believe bigger is better. Bigger isn't always better. Better is better," Rob says. "Where you find differences in the strengths of the firms and put them together is where there is true value."

Of course, there can be deal breakers among those differences. The cultures have to be highly compatible and the beliefs and practices of client service have to be similar.

For an acquisition or a merger to happen at anywhere near full value, the firm must be seen as strategic. We asked those collaborating with us on this book how they defined "strategic." The answers were very similar across the board:

1. **New service lines:** Can the business bring something new to the menu of services for clients? This is especially attractive if it can generate additional revenue, but it may be enough if it "merely" enhances an existing service line and better protects current fee levels.

2. **New specialist/subject matter expertise:** As businesses grow, it becomes possible, maybe imperative, to develop niche specialization to complement generalist capabilities. Rather than build that specialization solely internally, it can make great sense to acquire or merge with what has already been created. A more generalist firm may be very interested in a firm focusing on corporate executives in the high-tech industry, or one devoted to business owners, or senior legal professionals; the examples are endless. The transaction might also be driven by a gap in expertise. A firm might want to pick up a private equity, or an oil and gas expert, for example, in a deal to support its alternative investment platform.

3. **Location:** The acquisition or merger brings the business into a new geographic market, not only for attracting new clients but

also for broadening the base for recruiting talent and/or to achieve economies in situating certain "back-office" functions.

4. **Pricing and margins:** Sometimes the transaction can actually remove some competitive pressures, permitting more aggressive pricing. Or the acquisition or merger target may already enjoy pricing and margin advantages that, when combined, make the acquirer's financials look that much better to its potential suitors.

5. **Operational gap:** So far at least, this has been a rare situation, since most acquirers already have substantial operational strength. However, some deals have been done to resolve a gap at the acquirer—for example, resolving the acquirer's own internal succession issue.

At the end of the day, a firm may not need to be strategic to attract an acquirer, but it sure makes the process easier and the value greater.

Successor Considerations in a Merger or Acquisition

Before the 2012 NFL football season kicked off, the Baltimore Ravens and quarterback Joe Flacco couldn't come to an agreement about a long-term contract extension. Flacco didn't feel the team was offering him enough long-term compensation, so he ended the negotiations and made it his goal to have a year where no team could argue that he wasn't worth what he believed he was worth. This meant the end of that season would come and Flacco would have no contract to continue with the team. He could be injured, possibly ending his career. He could have a flame-out year and his value could drastically drop. Or he could have a hugely successful year and get a great return on the investment of believing in himself. Betting on himself paid off in a very big way, in fact. The Baltimore Ravens won the Super Bowl, with Flacco being named the game's most valuable player. After the season he was re-signed to a six-year, $120.6 million deal.

If you are a capable successor, recognize that you can be highly accretive to a deal. One of the ways founders maximize value is by having successors in place. The majority owners of a firm have strong incentive, therefore, to lock down a successor prior to entering into deal negotiations with an acquirer or merger partner. Again, if the majority owners want to maximize the value of the deal, having a successor in place prior to the discussions can produce great rewards for the existing owners—and for the successors as well. Successors need to evaluate these circumstances and determine the best way to bet on themselves. The successor will likely have two choices. The owners will try to lock the successor down before they go to market. The successor can either take that deal (or negotiate to improve it) or take his or her chances with the acquirer. If the successor is genuinely important to the business, an acquirer will place high priority on keeping the successor. Under these circumstances, betting on yourself and dealing directly with the acquirer might be the best the way to maximize both post-transaction operational responsibilities and monetary value.

Been There; Done That

Brent Brodeski, CEO of Savant Capital, has completed four highly publicized acquisitions over the past few years. We asked Brent to discuss what he learned in going through the process and what he feels owners need to think about as they look to sell their firms:

1. **Paying more:** Firms focus so much on the valuation's total immediate number that they miss the importance of specific, detailed terms and of maximizing overall payments over time. An acquirer will be willing to pay more if the owners are willing to be creative on terms where they assume more risk. Sellers don't get to have it both ways, whereby they maximize value but assume little risk.

2. **Yes, starting early does matter:** We've repeatedly told readers to start the process early. Brent offers yet another reason why: An acquirer will pay more if the founder and key employees are willing to stay on for five or so years. Coming to the bargaining table just as you are otherwise about to walk out the door into retirement won't maximize the value.

3. **Get your house in order:** If there are nagging problems within the business, clean them up before you try to do a deal. Smart acquirers realize that the warts you show up with will only get bigger postclose.

4. **Include everyone:** Acquirers feel more confident in a transaction where all key players are involved in the dialogue.

5. **Don't be an investment zealot:** Investment philosophy is important, but not that important. Expanding your repertory could be a good thing. In any event, don't die on the hill over it, if all other deal items are good.

6. **Be clear:** Owners who are able to readily articulate why they want to do a deal and what they are trying to achieve make acquirers much more comfortable. That clarity about objectives really helps to move the process along.

7. **Show me the money:** Don't say "It's not about the money" and then, throughout the discussions, make it all about the money.

Why Deals Don't Get Done—or Shouldn't

The primary consideration in any transaction, wholly internal, facilitated by outside capital, or an outright sale or merger, must remain what is in the best interest of clients. While founders and successors, and buyers and sellers are busy exchanging value and control, it's easy to lose sight of why the firm exists. Failing to keep that thought foremost can ultimately doom even the most sophisticated deal structure.

In writing this book, we were lucky enough to talk with some of the advisory industry's finest consultants, investment bankers, and private equity firms. These included Liz Nesvold, Mark Hurley, David DeVoe, Philip Palaveev, and Mark Tibergien. They all made the same key point: The number one reason deals don't get done has nothing to do with valuation. You might think it's all about the money, but, instead, the crucial stumbling block is the unwillingness of some founders to relinquish control.

Those emotional barriers are the subject of the final chapters of this book, in Section III.

KEY TAKEAWAYS:

1. Doing nothing cannot be a permanent, financially viable strategy. No one lives forever.

2. Don't expect perfection in the deal. There are likely to be some elements that any of the parties can find distasteful: discounted values; some degree of management intrusion by and some sharing of revenues or profits with outside capital suppliers; outright loss or at least sharing of control through a sale or merger.

3. Many firms will have the opportunity to access outside capital to assist in the transition process. This can be a positive or a negative, depending on the needs of each firm.

4. Not all mergers are of "equals," despite the publicity. The main point is whether life after the merger is better than before.

5. If you are going to look at an outright sale or merger, getting the firm's house in order and working through the deal may take longer and involve more mental and psychic effort than you anticipate—another important reason to start the transition process early.

Section III

EMOTIONAL CHALLENGES ... AND SOLUTIONS

Chapter 8

It's Not Just an Office

What you do speaks so loudly that I cannot hear what you say.
—*Ralph Waldo Emerson*

Probably everyone reading this book has seen the famous 1939 movie *The Wizard of Oz*. It's a lovely story about a little girl trying to find her way home to Kansas by traveling down the Yellow Brick Road, to seek the Wizard's assistance. Her good companions on this journey, Scarecrow, the Tin Man, and the Cowardly Lion, help Dorothy take on evil obstacles like the Wicked Witch of the West and her flying monkeys. The story, of course, has a happy ending, with Dorothy waking in her bed at home; the obstacles were just a dream. Given the way the story was told, viewers' opinions of the characters are pretty black-and-white. Dorothy, Tin Man, Cowardly Lion, and Scarecrow are good, the false Wizard a little pathetic, and the Wicked Witch of the West unquestionably bad. It's easy to have compassion for the "good guys" and zero sympathy for the Wicked Witch.

The Wizard of Oz was the first broadly distributed film to use color. The movie opens in Kansas, in conventional black-and-white, but suddenly switches to brilliant Technicolor when the tornado deposits Dorothy and her dog, Toto, in Oz. At the time of the film's release, audiences gasped in wonder and delight. We can't expect the same response here, but we do hope this book opens readers' eyes to new ways of seeing the opportunities of transition. "Toto, I don't think we're in Kansas anymore!"

In 2003, the play *Wicked* opened, based on the 1995 novel *Wicked: The Life and Times of the Wicked Witch of the West,* by Gregory Maguire. The musical has gone on to smashing success around the world. In October 2013, the musical celebrated its tenth anniversary on Broadway, making it the eleventh longest-running Broadway show in history[1]. This play serves mostly as a prequel to the story of *The Wizard of Oz* movie, detailing the difficult upbringing of the Wicked Witch. The audience learns never-before-told stories, providing a sympathetic framework for the life of the witch and how she became the evil person portrayed in the movie. The audience leaves *Wicked* with at least a modestly sympathetic view toward the witch.

This contrast between the movie and the play demonstrates a very important insight for the transition process. In almost every transition, there aren't good people and bad people. There are probably only people trying their best to run a business, to reach their personal goals, and, most important, to effectively serve their clients. However, at times, it's easy for all the parties involved to feel as though there are winners and losers, or good and bad actors in the process. Throughout this book we've told stories from differing perspectives and explored decision environments that need to be viewed through varying lenses. The same story, the same set of decision choices can look different when viewed through the founder's or the successor's lens of what's best for the business operationally or what's best for the founder or successor financially.

In this final section, we revisit some of those decisions and discuss new scenarios through what we believe are the most important lenses— the emotional ones. It's easy for founders and successors alike to let the emotional aspects get in the way of good decisions, cloud judgments, and maybe even lead to suspicion or contempt. Those transitions that are not successful tend to fail on this emotional plane. We hope here to identify some of the key pitfalls to avoid and some techniques to help all the players overcome the obstacles. There may not be a Yellow Brick Road and there certainly is no Wizard at the end of it, but there is some help along the way toward achieving the quest for a successful transition.

Know Your Personality

In Chapter 2, we reviewed the importance of founders and successors finding and building on their unique differences. These differences in skill sets and preferences can pave the way for an outstanding operational team to lead the firm. In a larger context, the complementary differences in the strengths of specific firms may make them excellent merger candidates. The differences in perspective of members of advisory teams can lead to groundbreaking technical planning insights for clients. Difference can build strength in all of these categories.

However, some differences can produce weakness in the transition process. One very important personality difference is the degree of emotional intelligence. This is not really a matter of how emotional or not someone may be, but about how well tuned in to this dimension of human experience someone is. In very simple terms, how well people recognize and react to their own emotions and the emotional cues of others defines their level of emotional intelligence. We've all had friends, roommates, coworkers, or family members who seem to know how we're feeling even before we do. We all also know people who appear to be "cold," unconcerned about the feelings and emotions of others, and seem to have no control over their own. Importantly, this degree of intelligence is about awareness; it doesn't say anything about acceptance. So, when you put people with very low emotional intelligence and very high emotional intelligence together, poor communication, or worse, is likely to follow.

This is not a book on human psychology. We don't pretend to have the competence to delve into this in great detail, but we do believe that it's important for founders and successors to at least try to discuss with each other the ways they feel and how they tend to express those feelings. Firms may decide that the best way to handle this is to do some form of personality preference testing, such as the Myers Briggs test. Others think it's best to hire a coach who can help all parties stay focused. We don't have an opinion on the best course of action. However, we urge you to recognize that failing to understand the emotional circumstances for everyone involved is a major land mine on the road to success.

The Office

Isn't an office just a place to put your computer and pictures of your family, do some work, and meet with visitors? Not by a long shot! The changing of office locations in a transition seems as if it should be such a small matter, but it's a great instance of the emotional freight that can be involved. It can also emphatically reflect some of the underlying generational differences between founders and successors. For many generations of business leaders in the United States, the "corner office" has symbolized power and status. The term "corner office" is a deeply embedded status symbol and shorthand reference for business success. Just go to any book website, such as Amazon.com, and search for "corner office." Dozens of books appear with "corner office" in the title, all of them referring to what it means to occupy it and how to get there.

So, having the founder—or successor—occupy the corner office shows employees and clients who's in charge. Austin Asset's founder, John Henry McDonald, had occupied the corner office for 20 years before the start of the transition plan with Eric. While the transition was under way, the firm moved to a new office building and John Henry designed his corner office just as he had dreamed. There was no immediate commitment to have that geography ever change. John Henry remained in the corner office while he gradually reduced his day-to-day responsibilities within the firm and the amount of time he spent in the office. Meanwhile, the firm continued to grow and needed to fill more and more of the space, often requiring the sharing of offices for employees. There came a time two years into the plan when the corner office was empty most of the week but the rest of the office was feeling very crowded.

For Eric, managing around this land mine was tough: How to ask the founder to leave his corner office, allow Eric to move into it, find

John Henry a new office so that the firm could convert Eric's office into a multiperson office? The first step was to present a real solution for John Henry that was "better" than what he currently had. Eric found a separate office on the same floor with its own lobby. This office allowed the firm to maintain the integrated technology, support, and close geographic connection, and provide John Henry with a flexible space bigger than what he currently had: a private suite. He was able to pick out the carpet, paint, and additional accessories that would go with the furniture they would move from his current office. He was connected to the firm, but in a new and different way.

Eric's second emotional challenge here was moving his own furniture into the original corner office. It was a surreal experience that first day of walking past his old office and starting the workday in the new one. The feeling of uneasiness was overwhelming. But the biggest emotional challenge was still to come. Eric needed to call a meeting with John Henry to discuss a business matter. But the question was whether to have it in John Henry's now separate suite or Eric's new corner office. The path of least resistance would have been to schedule the meeting on John Henry's new turf, but Eric concluded that that wasn't really the best thing for the business. So, despite his fear and anxiety, he scheduled the meeting in his own new office. Just sending that invite was scary. As the time for the meeting approached, the world seemed to move in slow motion. Just a few days earlier, the positions in that corner office had been reversed. This day, the symbolic shift was impossible to ignore; much like the deliberate planning for positioning at client meetings that we described earlier, positioning of the permanent turf carries deep messaging for everyone involved. The "occupation" of the corner office, in Austin Asset's case, solidified the irrevocability of the transition plan. Any opportunity for pretense, or backtracking, was shattered in that otherwise simple business meeting.

In Chapter 1, we told stories of founders starting their businesses out of their cars. Having any office space whatsoever was a major step in the evolution of a firm, so as the firm grows, the founder's having a corner office is a sign of genuine success. After years of working hard to develop a loyal clientele, build a sustainable business, and create perhaps many jobs, you can imagine what it must be like for a founder to step away from that location, especially if the successor will take that space. The office can represent the culmination of a successful journey, the realization of a dream. For many founders, stepping out of that office makes them feel that the journey has come to an abrupt end, that they've been rudely shaken awake from their dream—into a horrifying nightmare. It's no accident that many large corporations maintain quite luxurious offices, with full administrative and secretarial assistance, for retired senior executives. Those large corporate businesses can afford to provide that emotional cushion; most professional services firms, even big ones, cannot, so the psychic compensation may need to come in other ways.

Either way, the need is real, so it's important for a successor to understand: It isn't just an office.

On the other side of this potential psychological divide, it's also important for a founder to understand that successors may have completely different feelings about this aspect of the transaction. For some of them, it's often not about the office at all. Depending on the age of the successor, the office itself may mean nothing. For younger professionals, who have grown up in a high-tech, smart-phone world, the way to do business often has no physical boundaries and often very little adherence to "work hours." Many successors view responding to and initiating e-mail messages while standing on the sidelines of their kids' soccer games as being in their "office." Whether that is a completely healthy situation for the service expectations of their clients and staff or for their family and personal relationships—probably not—is not the focus of this book. For good or ill, that is the way things happen today. So successors might resist the physical move or even reconfigure the office layout to eliminate status-conferring private spaces. This, too, is increasingly common in contemporary office architecture.

Still, successors may come to better appreciate the benefits of that office, with or without the emotional baggage it can carry with it. And, in any event, if a transition into that special, high-status space does take place, it will emphatically say to them—and to everybody else—that they are now in charge. They have become the dog that caught the car. Now what?! So, now, pretending to not being separated, not being in a different status won't change the reality of having greater responsibility. That office might actually come in handy.

Successor Surprises

Well-known stories of successful internal transitions in the independent advisory space are hard to find. In part that's because there aren't many. The transition process for such firms is such a challenge that many firms just can't get there. The common default is a sale or, in Rudy Adolf's terminology, a "down the plane" ending. It's also because those internal successions that are successful often happen without much fanfare; they don't generate a lot of headlines.

One highly publicized internal transition, financed by the outside capital source Focus Financial Partners, occurred at Buckingham Asset Management. Adam Birenbaum, knew he wanted to join and ultimately lead a large wealth management firm, and he was willing to start by working in the mailroom, literally, to work his way up. He didn't start in the mailroom out of college; he started in the mailroom after working in his first financial job and after attending law school. Now as CEO of one of the nation's largest asset management firms, he serves, along with Eric, and not many others, as an example of successfully transitioning into the leadership position.

Listening to the interaction between Eric and Adam as they discussed their emotions in taking over leadership of their firms was one of the most enjoyable episodes in our research for this book. Anyone getting to the top spot of even a small firm has to be confident and ambitious. However, no matter how prepared Eric and Adam felt, that first week of running their companies quickly convinced them that running even a small organization is difficult and highly stressful.

One of the big challenges successors face is the need to lead, yet be reverent. Adam discusses this struggle: "Here I was now asked to lead the firm. I wasn't being asked by some group of random strangers. I was being asked by people that I looked up to and had the utmost respect for what they had built. I had spent years working hard to try to live up to their expectations. The emotional impact of now realizing these people were handing to me the organization they gave blood, sweat, and tears for was almost overwhelming." That emotion of excitement quickly turned not to one of self-doubt but to one of self-reflection: "I had to determine how I was going to walk the line. I had been given the position to lead and I had an obligation to lead. I had an obligation to do what was right for our clients and this came with the realization that we had to do things differently if we were going to become the firm we wanted to be in the future. As I was thinking about making changes, I quickly realized I was going to have to deal with the reality that I had to balance being respectful to the traditions of the founders with doing what was right for the business. This took some getting used to."

A successor's job is to lead. John Gruden, the Super Bowl–winning coach and now head analyst for *Monday Night Football,* talks often about leadership on the primetime telecast. He believes one of the biggest mistakes young quarterbacks make is to not lead when given the mantle to do so. If you are a successor, don't make that mistake.

A second major emotional challenge for successors in taking the top spot comes with going from being a peer to being the boss. Most successors had worked side by side with, and in some cases even worked for, people who now work for them. You quickly go from the person going to happy hour on Friday with your "work friends" to the realization that those invitations may wane and then end altogether, as you have responsibility for discussing their career goals, setting performance expectations, and determining compensation levels. Both Adam and Eric realized they had to develop an acceptance of the emotional impact of feeling left out. While not wanting to take themselves too seriously, both realized that their new responsibility to take care of the careers and, ultimately, the economic welfare of the families of their employees trumped their own pain at no longer being peers. There are now dozens or maybe hundreds of people depending on you to make the right decisions, in the short and long term, for the business.

A third potentially emotional challenge for the successor has some ready solutions. But those solutions may create wholly new emotional problems for the founders.

In talking with Adam and other successors, we recognized the commonly expressed need for and the importance of having one or more mentors, outside the firm from whom the successor can seek objective, unvarnished advice. For Adam, this was never an issue, as the founders of his firm encouraged him to join the Young President's Organization and paid for him to have executive coaching. He talks about how appreciative he was of the founders' encouraging this outside development.

It's difficult for a successor to be in this position with only internal mentorship. As we explored in Section I, founders often do, and should, want to mentor and encourage the growth of their internal successors. But at some point this mentor relationship probably needs to change for the successor to fully develop an independent ability to lead. That change, of course, has to be hard on the founders, especially when they are dealing with their other emotional issues. In Chapter 2, we discussed the impact on John Henry when Eric began to develop an external network. This change in their relationship was hard on both of them, but Eric came to realize that the clients, and the staff—and John Henry as well—needed him to grow to be the best business leader he could be. And that required him to grow his own support network beyond what he could achieve just internally.

This theme will repeat: When emotions start to run high, on either side, it's important to put the interest of the business and its clients at the forefront. Once that lens is used, the emotional aspects can more readily move to the background.

The Fear of Being Wrong

To be successful during transition, it's important for the successor to be confident but not overconfident. Rebecca Pomering, CEO of Moss Adams Wealth Advisors, cautions successors: "Understand what it will take, in the short term, to achieve the point of actual transition, but then focus on the much longer term after that. That's when the really hard part but the greatest opportunities come in. Transition isn't the end, it's the beginning! Be humble about what it will take to actually succeed in the business once the transition itself has occurred." Mistakes are going to happen. In most transitions, the successor is going to have to make big, and risky, decisions to take a firm to new heights.

You'll remember our discussion of the transition Austin Asset went through as they changed their advertisements, shifting from a picture of John Henry and his dog to the ultimate goal of a firm brand with no personal names at all. In retrospect, Eric considers this absolutely the right operational call, but at the time it was a big emotional exercise with no certainty that it would ultimately work. John Henry had to be gracious enough to permit refocusing of the advertising attention toward the firm and away from himself. This was a genius step for John Henry, but it also made Eric nervous. It was a highly risky decision to let go of what had been working, in the mere belief that a change was necessary for the business to really become enduring.

We are sure John Henry dealt with anxiety as the firm went from being his creation—and its identity being very much about him—to, instead, being about the (then very uncertain) future. For Eric, the process was not quite so emotional, but it was equally scary. When was the right time to make the change? At what point should he discuss it with John Henry? How much of a leap was too much? The biggest fear was that if the decision turned out to be wrong, the growth of the firm could be severely impaired. "I remember lying in bed at night, thinking, 'Man I hope this works!' "

The emotions on both sides need to stay in check as the firm changes. Founders need to ensure that they stay mostly out of the way while still protecting their investment in the firm, with the successor being empowered to try new things and make mistakes. In fact, most mistakes are small and capable of being repaired if need be. The temptation, on both sides, is to make everything a life-and-death matter. Almost nothing is. Everybody needs to keep things cool.

How do you keep your emotions in check when it comes to failure and decision making? As a successor, ask yourself two questions: Is the decision high risk or low risk? Is the decision revocable or irrevocable? Be careful of the high-risk and irrevocable category. As you start out, both founders and successors may be inclined to put many decisions in this category, but, realistically, not many decisions belong in that quadrant. For example, John Henry's advertising decision was a highly charged emotional matter for both John Henry and Eric at the time. It probably felt high risk and irrevocable, but was it really? Of course not. If it didn't work and the growth rate of the firm was hurt by the change (and that impact could actually be measured), the firm could pull out the old ads and start running them again before investing in the expense of a new website identity, stationery, and business cards.

Still, in those early months after the shift, the mechanics of responding to prospects had to change as well. The measurements of success had to be recalibrated. Prospects responding to the new ad would no

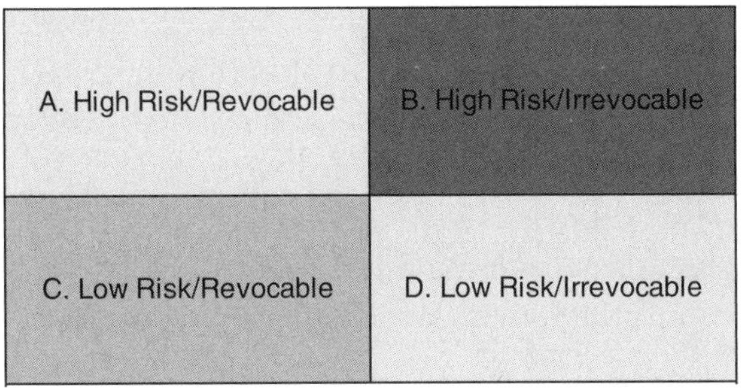

A. High Risk/Revocable	B. High Risk/Irrevocable
C. Low Risk/Revocable	D. Low Risk/Irrevocable

Figure 8.1 Risk Diagnosis

longer be meeting with John Henry. The responsibility to represent the firm and close the business fell, for the first time, on one of the other planners. How could they be even remotely as powerful as the founder? At first, they weren't; new business metrics declined, severely testing the wisdom of that decision in the short term.

The right decisions always look easy in hindsight. You have to make them in real time. Mistakes will happen, but that isn't the end of the world. Most risks don't threaten the life of the firm, and many things that don't work out as planned have some capacity for being undone. Figure 8.1 shows a chart to help founders and successors talk about decisions and what items should cause concern.

Quadrant C in Figure 8.1 represents decisions a founder should allow successors to make without consultation. Quadrants A and D represent items founders and successors may want to discuss. Quadrant B area represents items founders and successors *must* discuss.

Successors Don't Want to Admit Being Scared

Section II of this book was devoted to the financial implications of transition. Those financial considerations raise important emotional issues for internal successors that founders need to be aware of. Removed by perhaps many years, even several decades, from the founding of their firms, founders easily forget the emotions they experienced as they launched their businesses. Successors are face to face, right now, with their emotional responses to what can be a very scary financial experience: Will the clients stay? Am I good enough to run the firm as well as the founder did, let alone better? Will the founder relinquish enough control to actually let me run the firm the way I think it should be run? What if it fails and I've committed all the liquid resources I have and some debt on top of that to buy my way in?

As he thought back over the time of his transition, Eric had a deeply personal reflection. Here he was, in the shadow of John Henry for so long, he had to learn to deal with the emotional challenge of stepping up. He wasn't afraid to lead. He realized that not stepping up or shrinking who he was in order to avoid ruffling the feathers of others meant that things weren't going to get accomplished. There's nothing enlightened about shrinking so that other people won't feel insecure. Eric realized that, as he stepped up and found his voice, others were feeling encouraged to do the same.

So, while many successors are right to be at least a little scared, they need to get over that fear and convert its energy into a positive force toward their success. You can achieve success by running hard and fast both because of the attraction of the goal ahead of you and because you're trying to outrun the problems chasing right behind you. Founders shouldn't underestimate the financial fears successors face and should do what they can to provide support, internally or externally. Successors, in turn, need to openly acknowledge these challenges and seek appropriate help. It's not about either side being seen as brave or fearful, cheap or magnanimous; it's about achieving the best results for the firm and its clients. No one can win if the successor is scared to death.

In the final chapters of this book, we will look deeply into the emotional issues of transition for the founder. Most of the existing literature in this field focuses chiefly on diagnosing and then managing the emotional impacts for the founder. Encouraged by this attention, founders can become so wrapped up in their own emotional welfare that they forget the need to understand and effectively respond to the emotional state of successors. A successful transition requires both parties to get to some reasonably comfortable place.

Another important emotional factor some successors experience—but may not admit because it's controversial—is that they don't want their lives to look like those of the founder. It can be almost overwhelming for successors to witness the emotional struggles founders endure as they transition their businesses. Most founders have built successful businesses by making many significant sacrifices over very long periods of time. Many have made the business almost their entire life. They made the business the center of everything they did, not only in the start-up phase; they continued that devotion as the business grew; they never really let up on themselves. Often, that meant they were on the job 24 hours a day/seven days a week, developed few genuine interests outside the firm, and sacrificed relationships with family and friends.

We are not saying successors don't want to or shouldn't plan to work hard. We are not arguing that successors should get financial rewards without sacrifice. Some successors are just as much workaholics as so many of the founders, and no successor is likely to achieve full potential on the cheap. However, founders should realize that part of the emotional impact of transition for a successor is to feel free to strike a different balance than the founder did. This is not about better or worse; it's merely about legitimately different choices of where to strike that balance. Each deserves respect. The proof, as with any balance, is in the outcomes for the clients and in the ongoing strength of the business. As one of the characters in the movie *Friday Night Lights* says to his father: "I don't want your life." Many successors feel the same way about the founder's life, the founder's choice of balance, but are afraid to say it. That statement needn't carry any disrespect.

It's Not a Light Switch

If you watch how a person behaves over a period of time, you can probably guess how they'll behave in a similar future situation. People don't tend to change much.

The transition process often requires organizations to hit the reset button on how the firm will operate, how it will distribute ownership and cash, and how it will differentiate itself from its competition to be even more successful in the future. Many things can be reset and new thinking can emerge. Some things are much more difficult to change. Emotional characteristics of relationships are in that category. The views people bring to the table about each other, their views on each other's importance to the business, and how they view their ability to be business partners now and into the future are often already firmly set in people's minds.

That preexisting emotional landscape colors efforts to achieve the operational and organizational improvements discussed in Section I and the willingness to effectively negotiate the financial consequences of transition that we explored in Section II. Getting to success in these areas involves understanding the need to begin the processes early, giving all parties ample time to gradually carve new emotional landscapes. Founders cannot have the business revolve around them, as if they are the sun, and then, suddenly, one day turn to their successors and say, "I want you to buy in and start running the firm." The emotional divide, for both operating and financial purposes, is too vast. The best way for founders to navigate that gulf is to begin giving up operational control and transferring equity ownership, in small ways, without making a big deal out of it, before the serious transition even begins. That way, the successors actually begin to exercise areas of control and enhance financial wherewithal. Moreover, importantly, the successor sees the founder actually loosening the reins, sees the emotional barriers weakening. The successor, in fact, begins to feel empowered as well as promoted in the estimation of the founder, so the successor enjoys enhanced self-confidence over time. The founder cannot behave guardedly for very long periods of time and then just flip a switch and have the successor believe that, overnight, things will operate differently. Instead, think of replacing that simple on/off switch with one controlled by a dimmer and, over time, sliding that dimmer switch to the level that produces the right amount of light on the topic you are addressing in the transition plan. It should be neither too bright nor too dim, with the understanding that you might have to flex up or down during the course of the process.

The Slow-Motion Effect

We've all had it happen at one time or another. You see a glass as it falls off a table. You see a car crash as it happens. You see food falling off your fork onto your lap, ruining a nice dress or pair of pants. As this is happening, your brain slows down the view and it can actually appear as if the event is happening in slow motion. This creates the sensation that you could actually do something to stop the bad event from happening. Of course, the actual event is happening in real time and you can't move fast enough to do anything about it. The succession process can sometimes feel like this. Many successors believe they clearly know what needs to happen in the business but feel unable to take action. In fact, the question usually isn't whether you can actually do anything about it, but whether you reach out to attempt to do something about it.

It can sometimes be difficult for successors to recognize when it's an appropriate time to intervene and when it's better to just let things run their course. It's a little bit like kids playing Whac–A-Mole. But here the successors are like the moles. Understanding when to stick your head up without getting whacked or when to intentionally stick your head up to get whacked is an art that most successors should attempt to master.

It's important for successors to try to minimize the emotional aspects of the transition and keep themselves and the founder focused on the most important thing: what's best for the business—and for its clients. As we began talking publicly about this book, we started receiving calls from interested founders and successors, eager to share their stories and eager for previews of the insights we hoped to put forward. Eric and Jay, especially, got calls from frustrated would-be successors, asking questions like: "How do I get the owners to want to grow the business?" "How do I get the owners to quit 'mailing it in'?" "How do I get the owners interested in trying to take the business to the next level?" While successors can't, by themselves, make all the necessary pieces fall into place, they also shouldn't just sit still and remain frustrated. They have an obligation to try to do what they believe is right for the business. Although having different perspectives and priorities perhaps, that's what the founder, fundamentally, wants, too.

An Unfair Expectation: Successor as Advisor

In Section II we briefly highlighted a common, and problematic, issue: Many founders don't seek outside advice regarding their own personal financial affairs. But when they do, they sometimes seek it from the very people who are poised to succeed them. This seems logical to many founders: "Well, these people know the numbers and are good at giving advice, so why wouldn't I rely on them to help?"

However, for many reasons, this is emotionally unfair to successors. It requires them to force the founder to be clear on an exit date. No matter how emotionally stable a founder is, being forced to make an important decision when not really quite ready to make it could lead to a "shoot the messenger" reaction. There really is no good answer here for the successor to present. If the solution presented includes a transition sooner than the founder expected, then the successor can be seen as wanting to force the founder out. Alternatively, if the successor gets scared and shows a much longer time frame or uses overly robust growth numbers, then the founder might decide to stay even longer.

In some instances the numbers tell founders that they should consider selling the business to an outside party to be able to meet their overall financial goals. This could put the successors in a position of worry about their own future. Also, depending on incentive plans for a successor that would perhaps vest in the event of a sale, a founder may be skeptical of a successor suggesting such a sale as being motivated by the successor's near-term financial interest.

We recommend that successors stay off this slippery slope of attempting to advise the founder. It requires you to operate with one foot in the owner's personal house, which leaves only one foot in the business, all the while being suspected of having both feet in your own house.

Progress, Not Perfection

It's easy for successors to feel as though things aren't progressing. It's easy to feel that the stakes are almost too high in a transition and nothing is really going to happen. The stakes *are* high, in most cases higher for the founder than for the successor. Of course, as a successor you have a family to take care of, possibly a home mortgage to pay, career advancement to pursue—but you also have a longer runway. It's easy for successors to get frustrated because it seems like things aren't happening quickly enough. But ask yourself one question: Is there some momentum to the process? Everyone wants perfection. It's natural to want the process to that perfection to be over quickly. However, that's just not realistic.

We aren't saying you must wait indefinitely. What we are saying is that trends do matter. If the process is moving forward, even if it's slower than you'd like, well, then that's progress.

KEY TAKEAWAYS:

1. Transition is a highly emotional experience for both founders and successors; usually there are no "good guys" or "bad guys."
2. The "corner office"—or no office—is more a state of mind or a generational artifact than a real piece of geography.
3. Fears of general inadequacy, of estrangement from former peers, and of making a big mistake are special and sometimes surprising problems for successors.
4. Founders need externally sourced personal financial advice.
5. Starting early and gradually building the transition momentum relieves much of the emotional pressure for everyone involved.

Note

1. Jennifer Nason-Brown, "Long Runs on Broadway," Playbill.com, February 22, 2015.

Chapter 9

Breaking Inertia

The secret of getting ahead is getting started.

—*Mark Twain*

We are aware that many of the readers of this book are in very different places in their journey, but understanding what a good start to the process looks like is key.

When we had the idea for this book, Jay called a good friend who had published and edited a number of books. His advice was pretty simple: Even though this is a business book, you need to make it entertaining or nobody will read it. Great advice—although for the next hundred words we are going to ignore this advice and get academic.

What did most of us learn on our first day of high school physics? The definition of Newton's first law of motion: An object at rest stays at rest and an object in motion stays in motion with the same speed and in the same direction unless acted upon by an unbalanced (external) force. The teacher went on to explain that the term for this concept is *inertia*. Our textbooks used examples of runaway trains and boulders rolling down mountainsides. We memorized a few formulae in order to pass the test and never thought about inertia again. Eric still gets night sweats when he thinks about calculating force factors.

Inertia can be a good thing. It was positive inertia that catapulted John Wooden's UCLA basketball teams to 10 national championships in 12 years and UCONN's women's basketball team to 6 national championships in 12 years. It was negative inertia that Susan Lucci was nominated for, but lost, the daytime best actress Emmy 18 times before finally winning and that the Buffalo Bills made it to four straight Super Bowls, only to lose all four.

Obviously, the concept of inertia is more than a physics exercise. It is the strongest force our businesses and hundreds of others like them need to overcome to reap the benefits of a successful transition process.

Do We Have an Inertia Problem?

This seems like an easy question. Of course, if there was a problem within the company, the founder or successor would surely notice it. Tim warns that it's not that simple. Like many founders, Tim had to fight the temptation to do nothing: "Doing nothing is comfortable, at least in the near term. Choosing to change is risky and can be painful ... and especially so in the near term." Founders and successors are going to clash. This process is emotional and tough. The need for change can be realized only when a successor or founder feels pain or anxiety and decides to do something about it. Retreating to the status quo glosses over many of the short-term problems but in the long run damages the ability to emotionally address the needs of the business.

The Four Choices

The man who achieves makes many mistakes, but he never makes the biggest mistake of all—doing nothing.

—*Benjamin Franklin*

Founders and successors can choose one of four paths in the transition process:

1. Do nothing—intentionally.
2. Do nothing—unintentionally.
3. Do something, and start today.
4. Do something, but at a later date.

You are busy. You have a lot on your plate. You may not remember most of this book. Remember this: Doing nothing isn't necessarily bad, but it is a choice.

Is Doing Nothing a Risk?

Most companies are doing nothing about succession. Why? In many cases, the founders are happy with where their businesses stand. The stock market has risen since the 2009 collapse, and their firms' revenues have eclipsed the high-water mark of the premarket values. It is amazing how riding the wave can hide the lack of attention people pay to their businesses, and it is also human nature to not want to fix something that doesn't appear to be broken. Eric adds, "Where you are going could be more of an indicator of where you have been than where you want to go. In this sense, positive inertia could well be an accident, not the result of a purposeful endeavor."

Dr. Jim Taylor, a nationally recognized expert in the psychology of high performance in business and sports, talks about the law of human inertia: the tendency of people, having once established a life trajectory, to continue on that course unless acted on by a greater force. By our human nature, we are wired not to change unless it is necessary.

We believe doing nothing is a great risk, if it's not intentional. We also agree on another key point: It's almost never too late to start. In writing this book, we talked to dozens of founders and successors. There was a common theme among many: Both groups felt anxiety about doing something, but, in fact, most didn't do anything because they did not know where to start. A common feeling among founders was a sense of unfulfilled responsibility or even guilt. This is where inertia becomes a real burden, and doing nothing ends up hurting the company more than jumping off into the unknown results of taking action. Tim's been there: "You can feel stupid when a client says to you for the first time, 'What happens to your firm if you are gone tomorrow?' It's a question a smart client should ask and it causes an owner of a firm to do a lot of soul searching. It can cause you to feel guilty if you don't have a good answer."

How Does This Process Start?

There are a number of ways the transition process can start. For Tim, the need to tackle this problem didn't come overnight but over an extended period of time. He was leading one of the country's largest firms, reaping the emotional rewards of a highly regarded national reputation, and didn't have any short-term financial concerns. Doing nothing seemed like a decent plan.

The seeds of concern began to manifest when he sat at national conferences and watched advisors his age seem to be in complete denial about the succession issues in their firms. Tim thought, "I'm better than that—I'm not going to be the person in denial about not living forever, or not running my firm forever. My colleagues and our clients deserve better." Mark Tibergien makes the point even more emphatically: "Failing to plan for continuity is an egregious violation of an advisor's fiduciary duty."

These concerns, especially for clients, moved quickly to the forefront of Tim's thought process around succession. "I had made an implied commitment to our clients that our firm would serve them and their families for as long as they needed. The time span of their needs will clearly outstretch my personal longevity, but they don't have to outlast the longevity of our firm." As soon as the longevity of the firm came to the forefront, other succession issues joined the list. "I also had made an implied commitment to the younger people in the firm who had entrusted their careers to my leadership. How was I going to do right by them?" It was time to make those commitments explicit. More items were added until Tim found he had created a meaningful list of four founder issues:

1. How am I going to meet my commitments to our clients?
2. How am I going to meet my commitments to the firm's employees?
3. How am I going to leave a better legacy?
4. And, along the way, how am I going to meet my own financial goals?

Now on the other side of a successful process, Tim understands very well the emotional issues he did not fully anticipate when the process started: "The key to starting the process is having a really clear picture of what you want and, more importantly, a way to clearly articulate the motives behind that wish list from the outset." In other words, it is important to understand not only what this picture "should" look like, but also why it should look like this.

Can the Successor Start the Process?

Can a successor be effective in bringing about the necessary changes? Eric believes that, in most cases, change will come only from successors raising their hands and making the case for their future and the future of the firm: "Don't get me wrong, I'm not saying it's easy to get started, but if the successor doesn't feel sufficient 'ownership' to do something that the business needs, the business isn't going to get better."

The Homework Assignment

Eric was brought into Austin Asset as one of its first employees. He quickly passed the CFP exam and gained the trust of the firm's founder, John Henry McDonald. John Henry is an extremely good rainmaker and client advocate. He looked to Eric to assist him in building the infrastructure for the company to grow. As time went on, Eric became concerned. He was building a stronger, more durable foundation for the business, but with no actual ownership. He was making a conscious choice to spend his time on operational issues, versus building his own book of business, because that's what was required. However, without ownership and with no clients, despite his high performance, he was replaceable. Eric was building a sustainable business, and he felt he deserved to take part in the upside.

Successors are all at different stages in their careers at their firms, serve in different roles, and have varying confidence levels in their relationships with the founders. Eric cautions that if successors don't feel comfortable about starting the process today, they need to have a plan to get there over a period of time: You can't sit there and say you have no choice in the situation. To say you have no choice absolves the successor of any responsibility for the business. Clients and their families are relying on the future of the business, and the successor is a big part of that future.

How did Eric bring his anxiety to the forefront with John Henry? What was his thought process? He knew he had to get John Henry to understand four key points. First, he cared about him as a business partner and mentor. Second, he cared about him reaching his goals, but also had a responsibility to his family to focus on his own goals. Third, he cared about the clients and the business and could no longer accept the status quo because the status quo wasn't going to help Austin Asset meet their commitments to them. Fourth, he wasn't asking for a handout or charity from him; he could clearly articulate and show him the positive financial impact he made on building the business.

From Tim's perspective, what Eric did next was brilliant. The emotions of going through this process can cause founders to be unclear about their own needs and desires. Over the next several weeks, Eric worked out a series of questions he believed would help John Henry bring clarity to his desires. This clarity would be the seed of a successful transition process. He met with John Henry to go over his set of questions, delivering the message from a very nervous position, thinking that he could easily be perceived as disrespecting the founder of the firm. But the message was delivered from a place of genuine concern for John Henry and where he was headed. Eric told John Henry that this lack of clarity was stalling the business. Eric told John Henry that he cared about him reaching his goals, but that he needed to meet Eric in the middle.

He gave John Henry the questions and then asked if he would stay out of the office until he thought about the questions in this "homework assignment" and sought help answering them.

Jay also believes what Eric did was smart, but he points out the risk associated with pushing a tough conversation. John Henry reflects: "I am now deliriously happy with my current conclusion, but it didn't start out that way. I kept putting it off. I didn't respond well to Eric's initial prompting; it was not my proudest moment."

Jay believes a successor's role can be to bring change but is keenly aware that this isn't something the successor should take lightly. Timing is everything. If the founder is unwilling to accept that there is a need to do something, it doesn't matter how good the successor is in his approach to the process. If you don't get your timing right, you can feel like Sisyphus, repeatedly rolling that rock up the mountain. Successors should realize Eric's approach was right on, not only because he pushed the process, but also because he nailed the timing.

But how will a successor know the proper time? Eric points to the concept of emotional deposits. "Over the eight years there were many experiences in the company that proved my integrity and motivations. Each one was like a deposit in the emotional bank, and when it was time to take a calculated risk by asking John Henry to consider the list of questions I had made, I was essentially making a withdrawal. The key was that I had a large enough balance in the account to make a sizable withdrawal and still have something left."

At the end of the day, however, there is no genie to tell you when the timing is perfect. But one thing is for sure: It's certainly not "never."

Successors Should Ask Hard Internal Questions

As a successor, finding the right timing for the conversation with the founder is more art than science. However, we believe there are some things a successor needs to consider:

- **How long have you been at the firm?** If you have been at the firm for only a year or two, it's probably not the right time to have this discussion unless you worked with the founder in a previous role or at a previous company. In Eric's case, he had been at the firm for eight years before serious transition discussions began.

- **Can you quantify your accomplishments?** To be an owner in a firm, you must be accretive to the business. You should ask yourself some hard questions. If I were gone tomorrow would I be easy to replace? What have I done to increase the growth, profitability, or positive culture of the firm? Can I grow my impact on the business over the next three years? If so, how would I increase that impact? If you don't have answers to these questions that convince even yourself, you've got some more work to do before talking ownership with the founder. You need to sit down and reevaluate your goals and reassess how you are going to convincingly increase your impact.

- **If the founder says "no," what are you going to do?** Even if you can quantify your accomplishments and make the case, you may not get anywhere. What are you going to do if this happens? What are your deal breakers? In other words, what are you comfortable doing based on the founder's response? What are you not comfortable doing?

Going All In

Remember when you learned to dive into a swimming pool? Most of us stood hesitantly at the edge knowing we wanted to dive, but fear kept us from taking that next step. We finally overcame the fear and dove for the first time. But many of us got scared and lifted our heads during the dive, so instead of slicing into the water, we smacked on our stomachs, perhaps knocking the wind out of ourselves, and ended up flailing our arms and legs in the water trying to catch our breath. We then vowed we would never dive into the pool again. Of course we would do it again, and over time diving off the edge became so easy that we moved to the lower diving board, and then maybe the brave souls ended up taking on the high dive. What makes the difference in learning to dive? Eventually you have to have the confidence to take the plunge and go all in. You can't think about what might hurt if you make a mistake. And once you start to dive, you can't lift your head in fear. You push off the edge of the pool, trusting in the preparations you made for that moment, and you slice into the water.

Jay uses this analogy often because he believes it has parallels to the transition process: For the founder and successor to be successful in this process, they both have to be "all in." One party can't be diving, while the other one is still standing there with their toe in the water. Dive off the side and don't lift your head. Eric's story about a homework assignment to prepare for a transition is important because he made a definitive statement and showed he was all in. Guess what John Henry did after the meeting? He went home for the weekend, stayed out of the office for most of the next week, and came back with a clear vision of what he wanted in the transition process. He and Eric proved to each other that it was time to start the process because they were both all in.

Jay has seen firms where it hasn't worked and he believes the way the firms started was a big reason why: He suggests that the transition process that John Henry and Eric went through has two key items everyone needs to consider. They proved to each other they were 100 percent committed to getting to a successful end, and they had a definitive start to the process. It's like going to the Indy 500. When the race starts, you know it. Eric and John Henry knew it, too. If you don't get off to a good start, you can't readily count on a great finish. Some firms focus on succession only from the standpoint of the emotional wants of the founder. Consultants in this field tend to focus on getting the founder's life right. That's not really surprising, since it's almost always the founder who initiates and pays for the engagement. But, too often, the genuine needs of the successor can be left behind, and, worse, the successor can feel alienated and underappreciated as the one left to work, really hard, in the day-to-day business.

Sometimes the process seems to get started without the successor's involvement at all. Founders sometimes engage "strategic coaches" to facilitate better performance and greater job satisfaction. That could lead to greater awareness of the need for transition and greater facility in pulling it off. But there's a risk that it will never move beyond the needs of the founder and will miss the opportunity to focus on the overall success of the business and its future leaders. So, at least eventually, both founders and successors should participate in this coaching effort. Focusing too narrowly on just the founder can be a waste. Failing to truly engage successors can be a great deal more than an annoyance. Deep personal frustration, professional disappointment, and actual severe financial risk can enter the mix. In fact, a successor might be the best person to initially urge the firm to engage outside help.

Founders need to learn from the disappointments that are already occurring. This is fundamentally good business practice. Would-be successors tend to be very talented people with lots of choices they can pursue. Founders need to be open to seizing the opportunities the right people can present. If you don't show you're serious about getting the process started, you really can't blame people like that for not wanting to sit around indefinitely.

Tim suggests a balanced view. "Founders need to overcome their tendency to inertia and need to have a genuine, ongoing commitment to progress. But some successors need to learn patience. Some of these guys are in their 30s and don't yet have the benefit of understanding the pace at which tough problems sometimes get solved." We all agree that it's easier to be patient when both sides see milestones getting set and then achieved.

Showing Progress

An expectation of balance and the setting of milestones are extremely important elements when starting the transition process. Frustration sets in when either side fails to see momentum. It's also important to understand that momentum doesn't always mean the process is moving in uninterrupted linear progress. You can make good progress and then have setbacks. Getting the process back on track after a setback is just as important as setting the process on a good overall trajectory at the outset.

One word of caution: A lack of progress can just become the status quo. If sufficient progress is not being made, the successor might finally give up, fearing the situation will never really improve. To avoid this bad result, start with a basic set of parameters around strategic results so it's easier, on all sides, to show if the process is off track. As we describe further in Chapter 10, you can then pause and hit "reset."

This is about a lot more than being on good interpersonal terms. Lack of progress can do great damage to the business itself. Ironically, a stall in the transition process can become all-consuming and get in the way of focus on the success of the business. Important decisions can be delayed, putting everything on hold awaiting a clear view of what the future would look like. You can't let yourself get to this point.

Starting in the Future

Doing nothing, unintentionally, really isn't a good option. However, deciding to delay the start of a transition until some point in the future is not doing nothing. This can work as long as both sides are truly committed to that future start. But, Bob Oros warns not to squander the "gift of time." He encourages firms to start about seven years from the targeted finish point. Realistically, it takes about that much time, he believes, to unwind the founder's near identity with the firm. "Good market performance and great financial rewards," Bob says, "are permitting people to continue to ignore the issue; but time marches on and the options will get fewer."

The best way to prove to the organization that the decision is a real one is to ensure that the process has a hard start date. This date can change in the future, but something has to be circled on the calendar. Some organizations do not have a current need to deal with transition issues, and other organizations need time to prepare, even just to start. When you prepare to sell any business, for example, there is a step before you bring in the investment bankers called "transaction readiness." During this process, the management team cleans up their areas of the company, the board gets clear on the strategic endgames they desire, and a start date is put on the calendar. It's important to have a "transition readiness" step in your own succession process.

What's Next?

Getting started is one thing; overcoming the obstacles that arise as you move along is something completely different. In Chapter 10, we dig deeper into the idea of "founderitis," the emotional reactions founders face when going through the transition process. We explore the difficulties this very natural phenomenon can bring to the founder, the business, and those around them.

KEY TAKEAWAYS:

1. You probably can't get *everything* you want. As you go through the transition process and it gets frustrating, take the list you made earlier in this book, and focus on the deal breakers, the items you cannot bear to do without in the process. Everything else is negotiable.

2. Focus on the business first. If the business isn't successful, the personal wish lists are probably unattainable anyway. If both sides stay focused on the needs of the business, the remaining items should be less emotionally charged and easier to deal with throughout the process.

3. Set milestones. They may change over time, but set some timing guidelines on the process. Set due dates and hold everybody accountable.

4. Conflict is not bad. If the process starts without an understanding that conflict will almost certainly occur, the process will end with people not truly aligned. Conflict occurs because both parties care enough about the situation to not ignore it.

5. Set a social budget. Not all of these meetings should occur in the office. Go out. Enjoy the process. Many of the most successful transitions come about because business partners enjoy each other's company and develop a personal relationship built on respect, trust, and even, if you're lucky, friendship.

Chapter 10

Derailed

Waiting for perfect is never as smart as making progress
—Seth Godin

On the journey throughout this book, we have focused mainly on the many positive aspects of the transition process and the many great benefits of arriving, successfully, at the destination. However, as we near the end, we believe it is important to discuss areas where the emotional toll can lead to derailment. We hope the discussions in this chapter can prevent the train from going off the rails, or at least help founders and successors get it back on track if need be.

The Fear of Failure—Again

In Chapter 8, we discussed the successor's fear of failure. This phenomenon presents itself in the emotions of the founder as well, often expressed as an introverted reaction. Founders, scared about getting the transition wrong, can clam up and fail to communicate. Communication of the transition plan makes them vulnerable. It makes them accountable to someone, for something. It makes them feel that if they get it wrong, one of the biggest decisions of their entire career may be second-guessed by others in the organization.

This emotion is normal, but allowing it to manifest itself in a vacuum of communication makes the rest of the organization vulnerable. Founders and successors need to permit themselves to be vulnerable instead. Successors can help founders avoid this silence trap by encouraging them to communicate the plan or the process to the organization as a whole. Even calling it the "communication of the plan" might be the wrong way to phrase it, since it could connote that a founder and successor wait to address the issue in front of the larger organization until the plan has been fully formed and ready to be implemented. In our view, that's too late. So, while it's difficult, we think it's wise to be vulnerable, not yet fully certain, in the face of people who either work for you today or will work for you in the future. Talking through your concerns and acknowledging the fact that you don't (at least not yet) have all the answers brings clarity to the organization. Whether you're aware of it or not, they already know that something is going on—or they should. Perhaps ironically, that acknowledged vulnerability will make employees want to help and become part of the solution. People can only help fix the problems they know enough about. As stated in the THX trailer shown before movies, "The audience *is* listening."

Founderitis

As we saw in Chapter 8, successors have their own emotional hurdles to surmount in this process. However, they often have to take a backseat to those of the founder. Most of the literature on this topic and most of the professional commentary focus almost exclusively on the emotional framework of the founder. The guiding principle of this book is to offer a fresh perspective, primarily from the standpoint of the successor. Still, we recognize that the founder does have a lot to lose. So it's not surprising that, as if in a dance, founders' emotions usually lead; the successors' follow.

One of the biggest risks to aircraft pilots, even very experienced ones, is the loss of visual cues during flight. "Losing the horizon," at night or even in less than perfect weather during daylight, can cause the pilot to become disoriented and experience a vertigo-like sensation. The ground or water below them ends up looking similar to the sky. If pilots don't have or don't trust their instruments, the cues their brains send can cause them to operate the plane in just the opposite way of what is required in the situation, and eventually they lose control. This sensation is believed to cause many accidents every year, including some famous ones, such as the crash of John F. Kennedy Jr.'s plane in 2000. We believe that, much like the vertigo caused by a lack of visual cues for pilots, there are emotional pitfalls that can cause a professional services firm founder to have the same confusion in the transition process—and risk similar bad results.

Our good friends Keith Lawrence and Al Spector spent two years interviewing business owners and corporate executives about retirement and self-image. This research and the insights gained became the backbone for their book *Your Retirement Quest*. They were gracious enough to allow us to talk about some of their observations in this section of our book.

Lawrence and Spector observe that when founders decide to step away from the critical role they have played (perhaps for several decades), they deserve to live full and fulfilling lives. These entrepreneurs have spent their careers building their companies, creating jobs, and making a difference in their communities. Their determination and the inspiration they drew from ownership, combined with years of overcoming sacrifices, struggles, and setbacks, enabled them to build their dreams into successful enterprises. There comes a time when founders, for one or more of many reasons, ask themselves the questions: "Is it the right time to turn the reins over to someone else?" and "What's next for my company and for me?" Perhaps a different leadership skill set is needed now that the company has matured and the founder realizes that he or she "no longer has any really new ideas" to take the business forward, as Keith Wetmore, chair emeritus of the Morrison & Foerster law firm, puts it. Perhaps the founder feels burned out and is lured by the prospect of doing something different with his or her time. Perhaps a personal or family crisis forces the issue. As Lawrence and Spector did research for their book, they interviewed hundreds of Baby Boomer retirees. Since then, they've had the opportunity to work with thousands more. Their learning has been consistent. Many Boomers (born between the years 1946 and 1964) are unprepared for what is likely to be the biggest transition of their lives.

Business owners, like company founders and others who have linked their personal identity most closely to their work, are at the greatest risk of "failing retirement." They are unaware of the risks before them. For example, the highest suicide rate in the United States today is for men over the age of 70, who struggle to replace the purpose they found at work. The fastest-growing divorce rate is for couples over the age of 55, as relationship issues are heightened once partners spend more time together in retirement. Founders typically have not spent the time and effort developing a thoughtful plan for their retirement transition. And those who actually do some planning tend to focus solely on the financial aspects. In the absence of a plan for the whole of their life, retirees often find themselves floundering.

Some recent retirees still show up at the office every day, because they have not replaced the purpose, structure, and camaraderie that the workplace provided. Some show up uninvited for key meetings just to "see what's going on." Some publicly second-guess decisions being made by their successors. These behaviors can, of course, have a negative effect on the company and its employees. Perhaps more important, these behaviors indicate the negative effect that transitioning into retirement without a meaningful "life plan" has for the individual him- or herself. While these examples are, happily, not the norm, they are symptoms of issues many retirees have, especially those, like company founders, who were the most personally invested in their work. The key for any founder, then, is to build life planning into their overall approach to exiting their company and their former career.

Life planning can enable founders to be more mentally and emotionally prepared to close one door, as they leave the company they created, because they have spent the time and effort finding new doors to open. Life planning can be an exciting journey of discovery. Founders have invested much of their lives using planning skills and personal determination to build something great. They are justifiably proud of their accomplishments and of the legacy they are leaving behind. They now have the opportunity to apply those very well-honed skills and that same resolve to build an even better future for themselves and for others.

What's next? What are the new doors to open? It's obvious that changing routines and changing relationships can be scary. But it's scary for both founders and successors. Although the specific decisions will be different, of course, successors and founders may be able to more clearly understand each other's emotions if they go through the planning process, not just simultaneously, but together.

Life After the CEO Job

In some cases, the best course of action for the former CEO/founder is to simply depart the scene … permanently. Oh, there may be occasional visits to the firm to hang out with the staff and to meet with special clients. And appearances at holiday parties and maybe a summer outing are usually appropriate. The former CEO is usually very welcome as a particularly important person among the firm's alumni. But beyond those increasingly infrequent and nonsubstantive contacts, the old "boss" has definitely left the building.

This is particularly important if the old and the new boss aren't on the best of terms. The less the former leader is in sight, the better for the new one. Even on very good terms, for the former leader, the emotional void is probably easier to fill and the emotional pain (if there is pain) is easier to overcome if distance is observed. "Time heals all wounds," the old aphorism goes, but that's true only if the wound doesn't stay open.

It also helps if there's a new, highly engaging focus for the former CEO's time and effort and sense of self-worth. Maybe it's a wholly new career of board service or philanthropy or just having more time to spend with family and friends. Maybe it's an opportunity to turn a hobby into a genuine passion. John Henry, of Austin Asset, describes it this way: "I used to have a DCA—Definite Chief Aim—to have my firm be the premier financial planning firm in Austin; I was able to get over leaving Austin Asset, and be very happy about Eric taking over, once I realized that I had achieved that aim. I came to realize that I had a new Muse: the music that I could make and what that permitted me to do for kids. I couldn't be happier."

But there is another option. The old CEO may have a new, different job to perform in the firm. The old boss is no longer "boss" but has definitely not left the building. This was Tim's situation at Aspiriant. When he stepped down from the CEO role, he went on a six-month sabbatical with a plan to return in a new role. Believing that the clients would feel more comfortable with the long-planned transition if Tim was not permanently departing, the firm voted him onto its board of directors and that board named him chairman immediately upon his return from his six months away. Tim also came back to a new full-time job, continuing to serve key clients and developing conventional business opportunities with new clients. He was also tasked with leading an effort to build some wholly new lines of business.

During that six-month interim, his e-mail account was shut down and voice-mail auto-responses told callers only of his return date. Except for a planned, midcourse telephone check-in with Rob Francais, the new CEO, there was, deliberately, no contact with the firm. This was designed to give Tim an opportunity to get used to no longer being in charge and to give Rob a clear runway to exert his leadership throughout firm—a challenge made at least a little more daunting by the fact that the Aspiriant firm was the result of a merger between two highly self-sufficient predecessor firms, 400 miles apart, only 22 months years earlier. As Tim looks back on that now, it's clear: "The sabbatical should have been a whole year; six months was not enough. While I tried hard to behave appropriately when I returned and had convinced myself that I was no longer casting a shadow, I wasn't really fully accustomed to not having the power I used to exercise. And I think Rob could have used more time with me being invisible."

So one of the key lessons of the "new job" option is to build in a "getting used to it" period, long enough to manage the withdrawal pains for the former chief and provide a thorough shakedown cruise for the new one. A genuine sabbatical of lengthy physical separation might be best, though maybe a little cumbersome. But, however you manage it, the moving to a new job transition is not likely to be successful if everyone just hopes for the best by having the former CEO step down on Friday and take on new responsibilities the following Monday.

Another important lesson for that new job is to attempt a very delicate balance. That new job needs to be big enough to absorb the drive,

energy, and results orientation of the person who used to run the whole
show. These highly entrepreneurial spirits won't be happy merely being
warehoused. At the same time, that new job can't intrude on the prestige, prerogatives, and ultimate decision-making authority of the new
master of the house. The essential ingredients of that balance are advance
agreements on the specifics of:

- **The job's objectives**. They must be big enough, but not too big.
- **Decision-making authority**. Does the old CEO report to the new
  one, or is there some intermediary? Referring back to the decision-
  making options ("Rules of Engagement," discussed in Chapter 4),
  the "Keep Me Posted" approach probably works better for both;
  still, the successor has to be able to hold that founder/former CEO
  accountable just as they would any other employee;
- **Resources in money and personnel**. There must be enough to
  actually accomplish the job without absorbing wherewithal for the
  new CEO to set and pursue his or her own priorities.
- **Duration**. The new job may take a while to accomplish but probably should not have an open-ended tenure; at some point, the former CEO really does make an exit. In Tim's case, the postsabbatical
  period was just under two years, the last year being part-time. In
  John Henry's case at Austin Asset, the total transition period was
  seven years, with a gradual withdrawal along the way.

Given the risks here, why would anyone do this? Well, the expectations of clients—and staff—for comfortable continuity may demand it.
Importantly, clients superimpose their own psychic framework on the
transition taking place. Some are very pleased that the firm has built itself
into an institution that can easily survive a founder's departure. Others,
even before knowing any details but hoping for a particular result, will
say something like: "Well, of course you'll stay involved. And I'm glad
you'll continue to own a chunk of the firm so I can continue to trust
that it will operate in the culture you've created." If that expectation is
common among clients, perhaps the existing leader hasn't really done
the necessary job of preparing clients for a more significant change, but,
in any event, it can make a more complete departure even more difficult.

Finally, having that post-transition job may be the price to pay for
the founder/CEO to make a graceful exit. A completely "cold turkey"

withdrawal for some folks will simply not work. If you force that, the eventual result may be ugly and take much longer than it should, to the detriment of the business along the way.

However, there are positive rationales. The organization may need the expertise and client service effort of the former chief to accomplish the firm's business objectives; the overall needs of the business should always outweigh purely personal preferences. Moreover, the continuation of some highly responsible position for the former leader can be intended to demonstrate that management transitions don't have to be traumatic. So, despite the risks, a very public demonstration of continuity and collaboration can be intended not only to give confidence to clients and staff but also to provide a model for other firms to emulate. In the Aspiriant situation, Rob and Tim specifically engineered this form of continuity as part of the legacy they both wanted to create. But, with the best of intentions, this was understood to be an experiment. Not every element was perfectly planned or executed. Several years later, both might give it a "B+," but at least it was a plan—that they built together.

Term Limits or Planned Rotation of Roles

The difficulties of transitioning job continuity are often facilitated in some professional contexts by a set period of CEO-like responsibilities. Often found in large accounting or law firms, this practice acknowledges the job of "running the firm" almost as a chore. And, it's also often a closely constrained decision-making environment where the CEO or managing partner is merely "first among equals" within a small group of senior members of the firm. When the job is over, the incumbent often breathes a sigh of relief and returns to what is for many the more professionally rewarding role of directly serving clients. We've heard, however, that the retransition to primary client service responsibility can be extremely traumatic as well. The professional virtuosity that brought the incumbent to a leadership role can get very rusty while managing the firm's business instead of doing the client work.

This rotational or limited term approach has yet to develop in the independent advisory space. First-generation founder transitions are still only beginning, and we're not aware of anyone engineering a partnership-like, planned rotational structure to be the replacement paradigm. Where transitions are happening at all, one boss, who had had an indefinite tenure, is being replaced by someone else with the same expectation of an indefinite term. The public corporation model, rather than the partnership model, holds sway.

But even a successful first transition from founder to successor leaves open the question of how to manage the second act … and the third. Does it really make best sense to anticipate a long future succession of indefinite term leaders?

It's really no surprise that the founderitis malady is epidemic among first-generation independent advisory firms. The reasons are both financial, as we explored in Section II, and a matter of personal identity, as we've have described throughout this book and focus special attention on in this section. Partnership-oriented firms have largely immunized themselves from this infection.

On the financial dimension, partnership-oriented professional firms (that have endured) have done so on the strength of their client relationships, effective leverage of the labor of junior personnel, strict winnowing of talent so that only the strongest survive, and premium billing rates. That has permitted them to amply reward the current senior professional tiers, on a current income basis, while leaving room for successor generations of talent, eventually, to enjoy strong financial rewards through their current income when it's their turn to lead. However, that succession occurs, generally, without the additional element of a transaction of a capitalized value for the firm itself. This lack of necessity of paying for—or receiving—potentially very substantial capital sums can greatly reduce the intensity of the succession struggle. Succession may be easier when there is less money, relatively, at stake. As we hinted at in Chapter 7, this change in the economics of transition might describe the eventual financial environment for advisory firms' succession as well.

On the identity dimension, the psychic load for enduring partnerships' transitions is generally very much less. The names on the door are those of people who died some time ago. It's hard to imagine the managing partner of PricewaterhouseCoopers, for example, falling victim to a bad case of founderitis, despite the long-standing prestige, the deep client loyalties, and the substantial revenue stream at stake.

So should the ultimate objective of the management transition issue for independent advisory firms be to emulate this limited-term/rotational leadership responsibility? Maybe. It would require a fairly large firm, one that has grown in client revenues, resources, and personnel adequate to field and develop a deep bench of managerial talent.

But that very growth and that talent reservoir probably mean the equity value of the firm, today, is also large, bringing to the forefront the financial transactional struggle that is already so great an obstacle for many firms. Again, the best advance strategy seems to us to be the broad distribution of equity values, as early as possible, to facilitate optimal results not only within the ongoing equity transition realm, but also for choices among management formulations as well. Separating early the concepts, and the execution, of management and equity can, we believe, help to make the most of both and will be the best defense against ongoing cases of founderitis in second- and third-generation transitions.

Optimism Bias

Why do emotions get in the way of even starting this planning process? Why are some founders and successors not yet even on the track? All three of us have spent a lot of time with clients in our professional pursuits. We've found that most people tend to have a positive view of the world. Of course, people do worry at least a little, from time to time about potential events in their lives that would be very unpleasant, like getting sick or the death of a spouse. But overall they tend to view what is likely to happen in their future to be fairly positive. This optimism, it seems, actually is rooted in the way the human brain processes past events. Neurological studies have found that our brains allow us to perceive past events and project that view to the future through a phenomenon called "optimism bias." Tali Sharot's book *The Optimism Bias: A Tour of the Irrationally Positive Brain* details the practical application of optimism bias and how it drives human emotion and thinking. Here's one example:

"Having extremely vivid memories of past emotional experiences and only weak memories of past everyday events means we maintain a biased perception of the past. We tend to view the past as a concentrated time line of emotionally exciting events. We remember the arousing aspects of an episode and forget the boring bits. A summer vacation will be recalled for its highlights, and the less exciting parts will fade away with time, eventually to be forgotten forever. As a result, when we estimate how our next summer vacation will make us feel, we overestimate the positive. An imprecise picture of the past is one reason for our inaccurate forecasts of the future."

We believe that this optimism bias is also at work in the transition process—in keeping it from getting started. Many founders are too positive about the future, allowing emotional excitement around past success to paint a picture of the future in their minds that may not be sustainable. Much like Sharot's example of the brain remembering only the positive parts of a vacation, we believe founders can remember vividly the positives of past success and forget the work, effort, and hard days that helped build the business. This permits them to ignore the ongoing work, effort, and difficult days that someone else may need to accept to have that success continue. As the aphorism goes, "The older I get, the better I was." A corollary thought getting in the way of a successful transition might be: "Who else could be better?"

Reality Distortion Field

At some point in time during this entire process, the whole transition system may lock up, and it can feel as if a successful ending will never come. Founders tend to feel this when they can't get clear about what they really want. Successors tend to feel this when it's clear to them what the founder should do, but the founder is so wrapped up in emotional turmoil that the business imperative isn't obvious to him or her.

Regardless of whether the process is going well or poorly, most successors generally care about the founders of their firms and they want what's best for the business. They are appreciative of the opportunities given to them in the business. So it is especially difficult for the successor to witness a lapse in seeing reality on the part of someone they care about. The pressure of dealing with this frustration combined with the stress of trying to be an effective new leader in the firm can be very daunting.

In Walter Isaacson's book *Steve Jobs,* he describes the "reality distortion field" that surrounded the founder of Apple Computer. This distortion helped to make Jobs a great leader because he was able to make Apple employees believe anything was possible. On the other hand, at times this made him appear completely out of touch. Some suggest that this reality distortion field is a trait of many great entrepreneurs. Not overly concerning oneself with the risks of failure is a key component of successful entrepreneurship. However, it can also create a big problem for a successor in the transition process.

What are successors to do if they see the world a different way? As we discussed in Chapter 9, successors need to do their homework, assemble the relevant facts, and get over the fear of having a tough conversation. Tough conversations need to happen throughout this process. These discussions can be scary for both sides. The successor has to come up with a way to put facts in the face of the founder. Emotions have a tendency to get out of control in the absence of facts. While we were writing this book, we received a call from a would-be successor suffering tremendous frustration. His grief was based on the fact that the company wasn't growing and, in his view, the group of founders didn't really care. We told him he had three choices. Do nothing about it and just hope for the best (our least favorite), grab some relevant market and competitive data and try to have a very unemotional discussion with them, using that data as his guide, or decide it was time to think about working somewhere else.

Successors will be tested. There will come a time when the emotion of conflict will leave a bad feeling in the pit of their stomachs. A time will come when they need to accept the status quo or push the founder to put the needs of the business first. Eric ended up at a very important point within the first few years at the firm when John Henry was asked to attend a speaking engagement in Mexico, for which he was to be paid $2,500. The first question was: Is that personal money to John Henry or revenue for the business? John Henry decided it was personal money, which Eric was fine with. The fork in the road occurred when Eric reviewed the company credit card statement and there was a $600 men's clothing store charge. Eric asked John Henry what the charge was for and learned that John Henry had bought a new suit for the speech. Eric had a choice: He could say either "He owns the company so who am I to make a stink about it?" *or* "It's not right for you to take the money for speaking fees but still charge the expense of a new suit to the company." This was really uncomfortable for Eric, but he knew he had to confront John Henry about the issue. After all, he had been asked to watch the company books as if they were his own. It was a major turning point for the future of their relationship—in a good way. The company received a check for $600 from John Henry, and everyone moved on, with enhanced respect on both sides. Little did either of them realize the significance of this event until the eventual transition plan began to be crafted years later. At first, John Henry seemed to be relying on an expectation that the firm would directly fund the next stage of his life—in other words, it would be paying for a very large suit. He and John Henry now agree that if Eric had not challenged that small item years before, it would have been especially hard to challenge the founder's initial frame of mind about retirement.

The emotional toll of conflict can be difficult to manage. Even someone with very little understanding of the mechanics of a car, understands that a car cannot run at maximum RPMs for an indefinite period of time without the engine failing. So what do you do when the emotional RPMs hit these levels?

Hitting the Pause Button

Liz Nesvold jokingly says to get a deal accomplished, whether it's an external or an internal sale, requires her and her team to get "the leather couches out of their back pockets. More often than not, the reason deals don't get consummated isn't valuation—it's emotion. It's clear to the outside parties, but not clear to the internal parties that the emotional issues manifest themselves in irrational requests for deal terms."

Often, successors and founders attempt to negotiate terms based on their own fears—terms that can seem crazy to the outside world and to the other side. If both parties don't realize that their own emotions may be driven by fear or uncertainty, their "demands" may turn off internal or outside counterparties because those terms seem unreasonable.

Liz talked to us about the importance of sometimes just stepping back and hitting the Pause button. "Sometimes firms get down the path and they feel like they need to continue on the path just because they've started." One of the frequent instances of this behavior involves the founder's uncertainty about whether they have found the right successor or successor group. But forging ahead with the process under that circumstance could be a big mistake. Hitting the Pause button does not mean the process will fail. We've all worked on an important project that got off track but still had a good outcome after some reconsideration—and a little time away. Although only about 10 percent of the deals she works on end up in this "do or don't" situation, hitting the Pause button has mostly worked out for the better. Liz adds: "Recently we sat down with a founder who wasn't sure he had the right team behind him, at a time when he was trying to widen ownership and exit the day-to-day operations of the firm. Instead of pushing ahead, we stepped back and allowed the team to have open dialogue about it. It turned out that the successor had the same feelings and ultimately left the company. The owner took the time to recruit the right person and once that person was settled in, continued with the transition plan. The firm has grown significantly since, with a widened ownership group, and everyone is extremely happy with the end result."

It's important to manage emotions from the start of the process. It can be helpful to set out the ground rules. Who has the right to hit the Pause button? Just the founder or both founder and successor? When the button does get hit, will there be immediate discussions about why or will there be a cooling-off period? If the button gets hit, will there be a set time frame for resolution or at least to resume the overall transition conversation? We believe the proper answers to these ground-rule questions are straightforward.

First, both sides should have the right to hit the Pause button. Second, we believe strongly that discussions and dialogue should occur, but it's probably best not to do that immediately; both sides should take a day or two, or maybe a week before discussion begins. This is also a good time to bring in a consultant or executive coach if one is not already part of the process. If the founder hits the Pause button with no discussion at all, it can leave the successor in a sort of no-man's-land: "I thought I was going to have a chance to take over—is that changing? Is the founder now going to sell to an outside party and put me in a worse position? What did I do to make them question my ability and drive?" This goes both ways, of course. If the successor hits the Pause button, founders might wonder: "Did I pick the right person? Maybe I was wrong not to just sell the company outright and move on. Has the successor really bought into the transition process, or not?"

Some of these concerns may be valid; in most cases they likely are not. If these concerns fester long, however, it's easy to lose track of the really important issues of client service and the ongoing strength of the business that was (or should have been) the key impetus for the transition effort to begin with. So, third, if the Pause button does get hit, we believe there should be a deadline for restarting the process. Too much is on the line for everyone to sit idle for an indefinite period of time.

One quick, but important, side point about founders not getting trigger happy with that Pause button. Liz believes, as do we, that the current pool of qualified successors is too small for the future needs of advisory businesses. As founders wrestle with the emotional issues around identifying and cultivating the right successor, it's important that they understand that the pool of available talent today is far from infinite; they can't wait forever.

Necessary Endings

This may be the most difficult part of the book for founders or successors to read. Sometimes, no matter how hard we try or how much we want something, it just doesn't work out. It may turn out that the hoped-for transition of management or equity just can't be accomplished. It may be difficult even to know when that point has come; but at some point it may be time for the successor to leave the business, either by the founder's choice or by the successor's choice. This is a difficult event for all involved. However, it might also open the door to a much better outcome. Austin Asset provides an example here as well. Before Eric came on the scene, there was an earlier "partner" to John Henry who, unlike Eric, saw the firm more in a "lifestyle supporting" role. Eric, instead, was determined to make the firm a long-term, sustainable business, strong enough to serve clients even better and provide the financial wherewithal that John Henry was looking for. It was an emotional time for Eric, since this previously identified partner/successor to John Henry had taught Eric a great deal about the business; some degree of loyalty was at stake.

During a lunch at the "best sandwich place in town," Eric put the choice before John Henry—bringing a "necessary ending" to the earlier, informal, and unworkable plan of succession but creating a new beginning for a committed relationship between the founder and a successor who could actually make the business work on an ongoing basis.

In founders, you have business people who have been successful and expect to stay that way; in successors, you have people eager to make their own mark. In both cases, these individuals have as part of their DNA a willingness to drive forward, not readily taking "no" for an answer. Emotions in the transition process can cloud the judgment of even the most gifted businesspeople. So it's easy to see how both sides in a failed transition can be unwilling to admit defeat. Rationalizations such as "We'll just work harder" or "We'll just ignore this problem and try to focus on other things at the firm" can mask denial for both founders and successors. If you've already hit the Pause button, only to return to the table with the same frustrations, maybe it's time to go in a wholly different direction.

In his book *Necessary Endings: The Employees, Businesses, and Relationships That All of Us Have to Give Up in Order to Move Forward*, Dr. Henry Cloud lays out many of the reasons people cannot seem to move on from bad situations. He explains the difference between pain with a purpose and pain for no good reason:

"Life and business involve pain. Sometimes, as we have seen, creating an ending might cause a little hurt, like pulling a tooth. But it is good pain. It gives life to you or to your business … but there is another kind of pain, one that should not be embraced, one that you want to do everything in your power to end. The pain I am referring to here is misery that goes nowhere. That is not normal, and when it happens, it is time to wake up. It is time to realize anytime pain is going nowhere fast, a few things must be occurring … sometimes we are stuck for reasons that are truly outside our control. But more times than we realize, we are not executing an ending because of internal factors, not external ones."

In our travels around the industry and in our research for this book, we've seen many people accept being stuck. The successors feel as though they need to stay because they don't want to take the risk of finding a new position. They make the assumption that all organizations may operate the way their current situation operates. Founders accept successors who are not willing to go "all in" because they worry they aren't going to be able to find anyone else. This leads to an environment where a much less than optimal situation becomes normal. When we choose to do nothing about a situation we don't like, we are condoning it. It's a choice. But, in our view, it's not a good one.

KEY TAKEAWAYS:

1. Emotions are like all challenges in life. It's not a question of whether they exist, but rather how you will deal with them. Emotional conflict is almost certainly unavoidable in this process; plan to deal with it like any other challenge that must be overcome.

2. Make a plan, together, for whether the founder will exit completely or continue in some new role.

3. Consider CEO term limits or "rotation" of the management responsibilities.

4. Everyone in the transition-planning process should be empowered to hit Pause. If you do: Be clear about why and set a deadline for resuming serious discussion in hopes of resolving the concerns.

5. As a founder or successor, if you feel frustrated over a long period of time, with no momentum, maybe it's time for a "necessary ending."

Chapter 11

Building a Legacy

Being the richest man in the cemetery doesn't matter to me. Going to bed at night saying we've done something wonderful, that's what matters to me.

—Steve Jobs

To a successor, the emotional hunger of founders/CEOs can sometimes seem so great that nothing can satisfy it. Every commentator we interviewed made the same point: Founders are so closely identified with the businesses they've built, the cultures they've created, and the client relationships they've developed that overcoming their psychological resistance to stepping away is usually the greatest hurdle to success. Organizational conflicts need to be worked out, and the money aspects always need some agreement; otherwise, the transition either never takes place or fails in the attempt. But until the founder has crossed the "emotional Rubicon," as Mark Hurley puts it, there's no real opportunity for progress. So, while the emotional element for founders—and for successors—really does come first conceptually, the final coming-to-terms in the transition often requires slow and gradual progress toward emotional resolution.

Throughout this book, we've addressed many aspects of this resistance and the various means to achieve resolution. We conclude now with further thoughts on what can be the most powerful motivator for all parties involved: the creation and preservation of legacy. Legacy exists only if the firm has a future, so developing a clear vision for what that legacy—that future—should be can be the very positive goal drawing everyone's attention in the same direction. How that legacy will be achieved can be the vital task toward which everyone (not just the founder) can set their efforts.

The potential focus for legacy has innumerable options. Being the largest firm in a target geography—the most highly respected, the most financially successful, having the most prestigious clients—are examples of legacy goals oriented around the firm's prominence. Having the most comprehensive, most innovative client service offering or the highest client satisfaction are legacy goals targeted toward the service of clients. Recruiting the best human resources, being renowned for developing staff careers, or creating broad-based wealth building opportunities speak to being the firm of choice for professional talent. Jay recalls a visit to San Francisco in early 2014 where he joined Tim at a happy hour with about a dozen of Aspiriant's staff. Amid the drinks and jokes, it became obvious to Jay that there was a huge reciprocal affection between Tim and these younger people. When Jay observed this afterward, Tim reflected that he and his wife had never had children. "These people are like 'my kids,' I guess. I love them and want to make sure things work out well for them." Giving them a place to build their careers became Tim's legacy.

Many of these options, of course, would reinforce several other legacy characteristics, but clearly pursuing any one of them could be enough to fill the emotional void many founders are afraid to face. They don't really have to face what they might see as "the end"; their legacy can live on.

What's in a Name?

"A rose by any other name would smell as sweet." Shakespeare's statement in *Romeo and Juliet* has huge relevance in the world of professional service firms' transitions. Many of the thousands of these firms have names encompassing the proper names of their founders. Will those names live on? Not only is the existing brand identity of these firms invested in the founders' names, with substantial and expensive infrastructure (stationery, website, business cards, office signage, etc.) already in place, the founding individuals have connected their personal identities very powerfully to the identity of the firm. Having the firm's name continue—or having it deliberately change—is one of the most important and most difficult decisions in the transition process.

The proper conclusion is not obvious. Some of the most prestigious names in business, especially in financial services, the professions, and consulting, bear the names of founders, some of whom have been deceased for many decades: JPMorgan, Goldman Sachs, Deloitte & Touche, White & Case, Skidmore Owings & Merrill, McKinsey—the list is very long. If you avoid surnames and move to more generic or descriptive names you quickly encounter the reality that almost all of the really attractive names have already been taken.

This was the case for Aspiriant as it worked toward its merger of Kochis Fitz and Quintile during 2007. As David DeVoe remarked, "That merger solved a half dozen problems in one transaction." One of those problems was the matter of the name—but solving it was not easy.

Bob Wagman, one of the founders of Quintile, and Tim Kochis first discussed the thought of merging their firms in early 2007. In that first conversation, Tim set out a few of the "must haves." He would need to be the merged firm's CEO—for a time—to dovetail with the plan already in place to have him step down as the CEO of Kochis Fitz within the next few years. Bob nodded general agreement. Another requirement was that the merged firm would have to bear the name Kochis Fitz. Tim felt that, with its much longer tenure, its larger client base, and its long-standing history of leadership and undisputed prominence in the industry, that name had to survive. Bob winced.

As the merger negotiations progressed over the coming months, the working assumption was that the name of the merged firm would be Kochis Fitz, but the Quintile people were obviously never enthused about that prospect. Tim understood that they were justly proud of what they had built and were rapidly achieving prominence in their own right. The closer the merger closing date got, the more tense this issue became; at the signing of a final letter of intent, the issue was addressed head-on.

Tim recalls: "Quintile, reluctantly, agreed that we would go forward with the Kochis Fitz name as our opening bid but we would quickly reinvestigate that conclusion once the dust had settled on the myriad of other matters to be resolved."

Tim feared that the matter of the name would become a very long and uncomfortable battle and could easily put other issues at risk. He polled a handful of his colleagues and a few of his advisors/confidants, including a small number of clients with experience in branding and public relations. Their responses came down almost equally in opposite directions. Half said something to the effect that "you'd be crazy to give up the name—maybe the most famous name in your space." Others saw this as an opportunity to not only seal the deal of this merger but, even more important, provide an example of good transition strategy for the industry. "Tim, if you can give up your name, what excuse will others have to hold on to theirs?"

This last argument, appealing to Tim's thirst for being perceived, yet again, as a leader, won out. Tim's legacy would be leadership—not a name. The other Kochis Fitz principals, and, importantly, Linda Fitz, agreed that this was the smart strategic move; there was almost no resistance. Everyone at the Kochis Fitz firm was developing some level of enthusiasm for the merger, and the name wasn't worth risking the larger deal. As expected, relinquishing the name requirement and removing this irritant convinced the Quintile merger partners that Kochis Fitz was serious about achieving success. Eventually settling on "Aspiriant" took some time, effort, and money. "There were some very tense moments," Tim says, "and a few failed initial attempts, but we had all concluded that neither former name would survive. We were building the firm of the future and it needed its own, new name."

When Anne Shumadine and Susan Colpitts founded Signature, one of the first multifamily office wealth management businesses in the country (and certainly one of the first female owned), they immediately believed neither of their names should be on the door. As Anne describes, "We immediately wanted a firm that was about the team. The clients knew that it wasn't just about us as founders, but it was about wrapping a team around the needs of their families. Even as founders, we didn't own the clients. Signature owned the clients." When you talk with the team at Signature you find an interesting legacy story.

Anne and Susan not only kept their names off the door, they believe that doing all they can to remain differentiated in the marketplace and remain independent, as long as that's the best thing for their clients, is their ultimate legacy. Randy Webb, who was brought in from the outside to run Signature as CEO, talks about the role he plays in helping execute this legacy. Randy's comments show that the legacy issue isn't something just a founder deals with. Randy talks about his unending passion and the pressure he feels to ensure the legacy of Signature. He doesn't worry about putting memorials up for Anne and Susan when the day comes for them to move on from the business. He's fiercely focused on widening ownership, growing the business, aggressively planning for the increasing complexities in the lives of client families, and recruiting the best people in the industry to work at the firm. "I'm not thinking about what we can put our name on so people know who Signature is—I'm focused on making Signature the best firm in the industry. If we do that, our clients will walk around talking about us as being the best firm to serve their needs. That's the legacy we want to build."

What's Your Title?

Maybe a small point, but often very sensitive for founders and successors is the matter of title, post-transition. Does the former CEO/founder carry a business card? What does it say? Does he or she still appear on the website? Under what description? Is his or her picture in the reception area? What's the caption? Legacy can be supported—or diminished—by decisions on these matters. Eric reports that, for John Henry, remaining a card-carrying member of the firm was a big deal during Austin Asset's transition. "He needed and deserved to have a card that he was still proud to hand out."

Conferring a title such as "Chair Emeritus" or "President (Retired)" might fulfill the former leader's psychological needs. But having too prominent a public persona for the former boss could threaten the successor's actual or perceived authority. Drawing some conclusion about this is important, since others (staff, clients, and other observers) will form their own expectations and use their own terms. There is no right answer here, but better to have a deliberate, advance agreement on this identity issue than to leave it to everyone's guesswork. Keith Wetmore has found his "Chairman Emeritus" title helpful in settings where the leader of Morrison & Foerster wants to put the weight of that emeritus position to good use. Significantly, Keith doesn't choose those venues; the new leader does.

Although this book is about private business succession, perhaps this is an area where private companies can learn from the succession plans and actions of some of the world's largest companies. While some corporate governance activists are trying to change this, combining the offices of CEO and board chair in one person is still very common. Many CEOs of Fortune 500 companies serve as both CEO and chair. The transition process at these companies is usually many years in the making and the steps are similar throughout many organizations. The CEO names a successor and a transition date usually six to twelve months in advance. At that time, the CEO steps down, yet remains chair of the board for a period of time, often two years. Then, after stepping down as board chair, the executive is given an office and access to an executive assistant and perhaps support for a book or speaking circuit tour. This multi-step transition allows the organization to transition power yet continue to gain the benefit of the skills of the former leader and feed his or her emotional needs through a gradual glide path. Few independent advisory firms can afford something as elaborate as all this, but you get the idea. A completely "cold turkey" approach may not be worth the supposed cost savings.

Memorials

Creating some externally prominent memorial can support the personal legacy—or even be part of the legacy itself. We're not talking about erecting a statue in the entry courtyard. Rather, there may be some special charitable endeavor that evokes the founder's philanthropic preferences, or a named scholarship program, or a financial planning article prize, or an annual firmwide community service day. The opportunities have a vast range. This, of course, can be awkward for the successor. How much is enough to appropriately honor the founder? When does the memorial approach become an embarrassment for the firm—or even the founder?

We urge you to use your imagination to find a way for the founder's legacy to be celebrated. We've seen conference rooms named for founders. We've heard of a firm where the founder was a big fan of the New York Yankees. Although the founder did not request that this be done, the successor named the firm's boardroom after the New York Yankees as a nod to the founder's love for the team. Now whenever someone asks about the conference room name, it gives the company an opportunity to talk about their founder.

The range of costs here can run from almost nothing to potentially very substantial sums. The firm must establish its budgetary priorities for this as for everything else, but often a philanthropic focus for the memorial is something the founder is happy to support directly, in any event. The founder may be putting up part or even all of the resources, but the firm is creating the environment of recognition, gratitude, maybe even reverence. For most founders, that is more than enough.

In this vein, we're especially attracted to the named scholarship program choice. The industry has great unmet need for a robust pipeline of talent. The aggregate professional cadre is aging. For the success of these businesses in the long term, for ongoing service to clients, much more young talent needs to be recruited. If the current generation of founder pioneers can leave its collective mark by supporting the ongoing development of the next generations of people to serve clients and transition into leadership and ownership of these firms, they will have achieved a worthy climax to their careers.

The Finest Legacy

At the end of the day—at the end of this book—we need to acknowledge that, whatever external manifestation there may also be, the most important legacy resides in the minds and hearts of all the people involved: the clients, staff, founders, and successors. The knowledge that a valuable professional service organization was created, grew, and continues to prosper has enormous psychic value—for each of those constituencies.

The transition process is a journey; legacy is its destination, its culmination. Thus, this book has come full circle. Many members of this first, founding generation of leaders left very large organizations in order to build independent firms. They did this because it was the right thing to do for their clients. They believed there was a better way. This passion for making things better for the clients they serve has to live on in the successors who will run these firms in the future. This book was intended to explain why this transition is so important and to explore the ways to maximize the chances of success. Most important of all, we urge you to keep fighting for your clients' benefit as your primary vision of success. Here's to the founders who were inspired by that vision, at the outset, and to the successors who will keep that inspiration alive.

KEY TAKEAWAYS:

1. By picking a legacy goal, founders and successors have one more opportunity to position the transition as, not the end, but just the beginning for the founder.
2. Don't underestimate the importance of the name on the door.
3. A successor can help the emotional reaction of the founder by finding the right job title and role after the transition is complete.
4. We believe firms can honor founders and solve the needs of the industry through named scholarship programs.
5. The greatest founder legacy is the knowledge that the firm that was built from virtually nothing continues to give people jobs and continues to enhance the lives of its clients.

Some Final Words

As we wrote this book, many people asked, "Why are you doing this?" There are two reasons. First, we believe that there has been a voice missing in the whole transition story—the voice of the successor. We have tried to present a thorough picture of the organizational, financial, and emotional dimensions of management and ownership succession, with a view balanced between the legitimate concerns, fears, expectations, and hopes of both sides of this necessary transition. Where we've had to make a choice, where we've had to express a preference, we've nodded in favor of the successors in order to encourage their voice for the future of their firms, to build legacies that duly honor the founders. All of that is to support the second reason for the book: the benefit to clients. In some important sense, these transitions are about leaving the past behind and looking to the future—and especially to a better future for clients. Their future needs to trump anyone's past.

This is not to say that irresolvable conflicts between founders and successors must occur. On the contrary, the goal of this book has been to help all parties avoid those conflicts altogether or comfortably resolve them when they do arise. We trust that the learnings shared in this book will ease the pressure for everyone involved and help create much greater clarity for the tidal wave of transitions to come. Nor is this to say that the past and the future can never collaborate. In fact, they do; the future is at least in large part a function of the past. But where there may be no way to comfortably resolve some conflict or where the future truly needs to depart from the past in order to benefit clients, we vote in favor of that change.

Throughout the world, the number of individuals served by independent advisory firms is measured in the many millions, perhaps even the hundreds of millions. They include the widows getting unbiased advice about making ends meet; they are the young workers getting advice about savings and investments; they are the well-to-do learning how to maximize their philanthropy; they are the young, growing families served by the wealth advisor in their own community whose kids go to school with their kids. Most of these clients are best served, not by the largest multinational financial services firms, whose offerings are often inherently conflicted, but by independent firms with local culture, strong client service focus, and durable relationships of personal trust.

These clients will suffer if these independent firms do not transition their management and ownership well. We are at the threshold of the first generation of founders being about to move on. We are seeing the emergence of the first generation of talented professionals eager to take their place. Without careful strategy, without a commitment to fairness, and without at least a little good luck, these businesses could cease to exist or might be forced to consolidate into something like—or sell to—the very firms clients are trying to avoid. So this effort is about much more than making the best deal between specific parties to a transaction; successful transition of these advisory businesses is very important to the actual financial health and to the peace of mind of many millions of current and potential future clients around the globe. If we've been even a little helpful in bringing that about, we will have accomplished everything we set out to do.

The independent advisory space will, of course, continue to evolve in the coming years. Many smaller accounting firms may be forced to merge; law firms may face increasing pricing pressure; wealth management firms will be hit by rising regulatory costs and will have to come to grips with changing business models forced—or facilitated—by new, low-cost, and highly efficient competitors for some of their current services (think "robo advisors").

This leads some to ask whether the future of advisory businesses can be as good as the past. The only thing for sure is that it will be different. But, of course, the future can be even brighter; for the sake of clients, we should all strive to make it so. The independent advisory business sector was built initially on the opportunity to solve problems for clients that others could not or would not solve. In a financial environment that is becoming increasingly complex and globalized there are more opportunities to solve client problems now than ever before. Continuing to respond well to clients' needs will take a successor generation that perhaps thinks differently and a founder generation that allows its businesses to head down somewhat different paths. We are confident such entrepreneurial successors exist, in large numbers, and we are confident that the fundamental willingness of founders to let successors "make it up as they go along" is still alive and well.

Now go unlock your future!

Bibliography

Aronoff, Craig E., and John L. **Ward**. *Preparing Successors for Leadership: Another Kind of Hero*. New York: Palgrave Macmillan, 2011.

Brown, Brene. *Daring Greatly: How the Courage to Be Vulnerable Transforms the Way We Live Love, Parent and Lead*. New York: Gotham Books, 2012.

Cloud, Henry. *Necessary Endings: The Employees, Businesses, and Relationships That All of Us Have to Give Up in Order to Move Forward*. New York: HarperCollins, 2011.

Covey, Stephen R. *Seven Habits of Highly Effective People*. New York: Simon & Schuster, 2013.

Dotlich, David L., and Peter C. **Cairo**. *Why CEOs Fail: The 11 Behaviors That Can Derail Your Climb to the Top*. Hoboken, NJ: John Wiley & Sons, 2007.

Ellis, Charles D. *What It Takes: Seven Secrets of Success from the World's Greatest Professional Firms*. Hoboken, NJ: John Wiley & Sons, 2013.

Isaacson, Walter. *Steve Jobs*. New York: Simon & Schuster, 2011.

Klein, Gary. *Seeing What Others Don't: The Remarkable Ways We Gain Insights*. Philadelphia, PA: Perseus Books, 2013.

Krystee, Kaycee, with Michael **Moser**. *Wealth Regeneration at Retirement: Planning for a Lifetime of Leadership*. Hoboken, NJ: John Wiley & Sons, 2012.

Lawrence, Keith, and Alan **Spector**. *Your Retirement Quest, Parts 1 and 2*. Cincinnati, OH: Cincinnati Publishing, 2010 and 2014.

Piven, Peter, with William **Mandel**. *Architect's Essentials of Ownership Transition.* Hoboken, NJ: John Wiley & Sons, 2002.

Sharot, Tali. *The Optimism Bias: A Tour of the Irrationally Positive Brain.* New York: Pantheon, 2011.

Sonnenfeld, Jeffrey. *The Hero's Farewell: What Happens When CEOs Retire.* New York: Oxford University Press, 1988.

Stengel, Jim. *Grow: How Ideals Power Growth and Profit at the World's Greatest Companies.* New York: Crown Business, 2011.

Supplemental Material

Client Touchpoint Exercise

Goal: To determine the current and future responsibilities for key client interactions.

The In-Office Meeting	Who	When	Comments
Greet when they arrive			
Take order for drinks			
Take coats			

Outside-the-Office Meeting

Scheduling a meeting			
Information requests—need information from client			
Holding client accountable for their tasks			
Updating client on tasks completed for them			

Consistent Communication:

Market commentaries			
Company newsletters			
Holiday cards			

Social Meetings:

Scheduling a social event			
Attending the social event			

Client Touchpoint Exercise

To determine the current and future responsibilities for key client interactions.

The In-Office Meeting:

	Who	When	Comments

Outside-the-Office Meeting:

Consistent Communication:

Social Meetings:

Human Capital Framework

Goal: As the founder is removed, the successor will have to make hard people decisions. This framework aims to depersonalize the human capital element as much as possible.

	John XYZ	Katie ABC			
Hire again?	Yes	No			
Can the person grow?	Yes	Yes			
Future best in class?	Maybe	No			
Position critical?	Yes	No			

Human Capital Framework

As the founder is removed, the successor will have to make hard people decisions. This framework aims to depersonalize the human capital element as much as possible.

Hire again?					
Can the person grow?					
Future best in class?					
Position critical?					

Role Transition Matrix

Goal: To set the stage for discussions between founders and successors around current-day responsibilities and future transition points of the day-to-day activities.

	Items Completed Today	Stop/Start/Continue	When	To/From	Training Needed
Founder	Chair Investment Committee	Continue	For 1 year	Successor	Yes
	Meet with small prospects	Stop	Next 60 days	Founder	No
	Chair Advisory Board	Start	Next 90 days	N/A	N/A

	Items Completed Today	Stop/Start/Continue	When	To/From	Training Needed
Successor	Meet with small prospects	Start	Next 60 days	Founder	No
	Train junior analysts	Stop	Next 90 days	Successor	Yes
	Attend meetings with founder	Continue	For 1 year	N/A	Yes

Role Transition Matrix

To set the stage for discussions between founders and successors around current day responsibilities and future transition points of the day-to-day activities.

	Items Completed Today	Stop/Start/ Continue	When	To/From	Training Needed
Founder	Chair Investment Committee				
	Meet with small prospects				
	Chair Advisory board				

Successor	Meet with small prospects				
	Train junior analysts				
	Attend meetings with Founder				

Pie-Splitting Exercise

Goal: Provide a way for successors and founders to work through the difficult task of fairly splitting equity and cash for past created value and future created value.

This is intended to merely be illustrative of the kind of *fairness* conversation that **all** parties, in **all** sizes of firms, with **all** forms of transition strategies need to engage in.

Equity Value: What's Been Created

Revenue	$1,000,000
Profit	$400,000
Valuation method	Earnings multiple
Factor	6.5
Total value	$2,600,000
Split: 90% founder	**$2,340,000**
Split: 10% successor	**$260,000**

Equity Value: Future Value Created

	Today	+1 Year	+2 Years	+3 Years	Change
Revenue	$1,000,000	$1,100,000	$1,210,000	$1,331,000	$331,000
Profits	$400,000	$440,000	$484,000	$532,400	$132,400
Valuation method	Earnings multiple				
Factor	6.5	6.5	6.5	6.5	
Growth rate	10%				
Value	$2,600,000	$2,860,000	$3,146,000	$3,460,600	**$860,600**

Split: 30% founder	**$258,180**
Split: 70% successor	**$602,420**

Cash Splits

Revenue	$1,000,000
FCBOC (1)	$750,000
Founder compensation	$150,000
Successor compensation	$200,000
Ownership pool	$400,000
Split: 90% founder	$360,000
Split: 10% successor	$40,000

Business value	$2,600,000
ROR for ownership*	15%
ROR target	12%
Difference	3%

*Cash ROR.

Step 1: Calculate free cash flow before owners compensation: Represents the cash present (excluding non-cash items: depreciation, amortization, etc.) prior to owners receiving any cash for job responsibitlies or ownership.

Step 2: Determine the compensation founder and successor each receive for their day-to-day job responsibilities.

Step 3: Calculate the ownership pool. Determine the size of the ownership distribution pool.

Step 4: Calculate potential distributions as well as rate of return on ownership.

Step 5: Determine a rate of return for ownership target: in this case we used 12 percent.

Step 6: Determine if current return is below or above target.

Step 7: If rate of return is above target, determine if difference will be reinvested or distributed (in this case 3 percent above target).

Pie Splitting Exercise

Provide a way for successors and founders to work through the difficult task of fairly splitting equity and cash for past created value and future created value.

This is intended to merely be illustrative of the kind of *fairness* conversation that **all** parties, in **all** sized firms, with **all** forms of transition strategies need to engage in.

Equity Value: What's Been Created

Revenue	
Profit	
Valuation method	
Factor	
Total value	
Split: % founder	
Split: % successor	

Equity Value: Future Value Created

	Today	+1 Year	+2 Years	+3 Years	Change
Revenue					
Profits					
Valuation method					
Factor					
Growth rate					
Value	$ -	$ -	$ -	$ -	$ -

Split: % founder	$ -
Split: % successor	$ -

Cash Splits

Revenue	
FCBOC (1)	
Founder compensation	
Successor compensation	
Ownership pool	
Split: 90% founder	
Split: 10% successor	

Business value	
ROR for ownership*	
ROR target	
Difference	

*Cash ROR.

Step 1: Calculate free cash flow before owners compensation (FCBOC): Represents the cash present (excluding non-cash items: depreciation, amortization, etc.) prior to owners receiving any cash for job responsibitlies or ownership.

Step 2: Determine the compensation founder and successor each receive for their day-to-day job responsibilities.

Step 3: Calculate the ownership pool. Determine the size of the ownership distribution pool.

Step 4: Calculate potential distributions as well as rate of return (ROR) on ownership.

Step 5: Determine a rate of return for ownership target.

Step 6: Determine if current return is below or above target.

Step 7: If rate of return is above target, determine if difference will be reinvested or distributed.

Improvement Matrix

Goal: Identify the cause of less than optimal results in the business to make changes for future success.

Issue	Company Problem	Experience Gap	Skills Gap	Execution Flaw	What's Next?
Receptionist not getting in by 8 A.M.					
Intern messes up data analysis					

Improvement Matrix

Identify the cause of less than optimal results in the business to make changes for future success.

Issue	Company Problem	Experience Gap	Skills Gap	Execution Flaw	What's Next?

Interviewee Biographies

Rudy Adolf, CEO, Focus Financial

Rudy founded Focus Financial Partners in 2006 to provide independent, entrepreneurial RIAs with strategic support for growth and succession planning while retaining their autonomy to continue to do what made them successful in the past. With Focus's success in the RIA space, the firm subsequently launched Focus Connections and Focus Successions®, programs aimed to solve the two biggest challenges in the industry: broker teams going independent and looking to transition to a fiduciary model and RIAs without robust business continuity plans.

Focus is the leading international partnership of independent fiduciary wealth management firms, with over 30 partner firms and more than $325 million in revenues. Focus is recognized as the market leader and has consistently been named as one of *Inc. Magazine*'s and Crain's fastest-growing companies in the United States.

Prior to founding Focus, Rudy held senior leadership positions at American Express and was a partner at McKinsey.

Chris Benson, CPA/PFS, L.K. Benson & Company

Chris Benson joined his father's firm in May 2009 after spending five years with a national CPA firm. He is a CPA, with a master's degree in taxation from the University of Baltimore and has passed the Personal Financial Specialist exam through the AICPA. Chris's primary responsibilities include working with clients in the tax, personal financial planning, and investment planning areas. Chris leads the AICPA PFP Section's efforts with emerging leaders in the CPA financial planning profession. He and his father expect Chris to eventually take responsibility for management of the company.

Lyle Benson, CPA/PFS, CFP, L.K. Benson & Company

Lyle K. Benson, Jr., is founder and president of L.K. Benson & Company, a CPA/financial planning firm based in Baltimore, Maryland, since 1994 specializing in personal financial planning, tax, and investment advisory services for high-income individuals, corporate executives, and business owners across the country.

Lyle's career spans more than 30 years, including numerous leadership positions in the AICPA PFP Division Executive Committee, National Accreditation Committee (AICPA), and Baltimore Association for Financial Planning. Lyle helped to found the Association of CPA Financial Planners (an organization of PFS) and serves on the CCH Tax and Estate Planning Advisory Board. He developed and taught a graduate-level course in personal financial planning at the University of Baltimore.

Adam Birenbaum, CEO, Buckingham

Adam Birenbaum is CEO of Buckingham and BAM Advisor Services, one of the leading independent wealth management firms in the United States. Under Adam's leadership, Buckingham and BAM serve more than 17,000 clients around the country, providing comprehensive financial planning and evidence-based investment strategies to individuals and families, institutions, retirement plans, and healthcare practice owners. Collectively, the organization manages or administers more than $24 billion in assets. With a keen focus on a combination of organic and acquisition-based growth strategies, Buckingham has created experienced wealth management teams and has evolved both the depth and breadth of the client experience.

Brent Brodeski, CEO, Savant

Brent is the chief executive officer, a principal, and one of the financial advisors for the clients of Savant, having joined the firm in 1992. He has been involved in the financial services industry since 1988 and has previously taught investment and finance courses at colleges and universities in northern Illinois. Brent is a cofounder and past president of Zero Alpha Group (ZAG), an industry association. He is also a cofounder of the Alliance for RIAs (aRIA), a prestigious industry group that together manages over $20 billion.

Savant was founded in 1986 and combined with The Monitor Group in 2012. The founding impetus was a frustration with the way financial services were traditionally offered: suspicious advice given away for "free" in exchange for the sale of a commissioned product. Savant is consistently ranked on Barron's list of the nation's top 100 wealth management firms.

David J. Cassady, CPA, Cassady Schiller & Associates

David Cassady cofounded Cassady Schiller and Associates in Cincinnati, Ohio, in 1990. David specializes in providing accounting, tax, and business advisory services to family-held businesses, their owners, and other high-net-worth individuals. David has extensive experience in the areas of business tax planning and consulting, compensation planning, succession planning, and mergers and acquisitions.

With more than 34 years experience, David's approach to client service and relationships has encompassed a trusting, creative, and proactive strategy to help his clients, their businesses, and families maximize their personal and economic goals. He currently serves the firm as managing partner.

Bernard J. Clark, Executive Vice President, Schwab

Bernie Clark is head of Schwab Advisor Services, the business that provides custodial, operational, and trading support to nearly 7,000 independent investment advisory firms with more than $1 trillion in assets under management. It also provides practice management and consultative support to help independent investment advisors start, build, and grow their firms, with training and consultation in the succession and mergers and acquisition arenas.

A recognized industry leader, Bernie has been ranked by *Investment Advisor* magazine as one of the 25 most influential people in the industry. He has more than 30 years of financial industry experience serving individual and institutional investors. He began his career at Schwab in 1998 as senior vice president of trading and operations for Schwab Institutional, the predecessor group serving the RIA community. He took on his current role as head of Schwab Advisor Services in 2010.

Bill Crager, President, Envestnet

Bill Crager is president of Envestnet and has been with the company since its founding in 2000. He leads Envestnet's platform, product, and relationship management efforts. Prior to joining Envestnet, Crager served as managing director at Nuveen Investments beginning in 1997 and prior to that for Rittenhouse Financial Services, a leader in the managed account industry. In 2015, he received the Pioneer Award from the Money Management Institute, the national association representing the $4 trillion management investment solutions and wealth management industry. The Pioneer Award is given to an individual who serves as an advocate and catalyst for the growth of the managed investment solutions and wealth management industry.

David DeVoe, Managing Partner, DeVoe and Company

David DeVoe has been a major force in RIA transition planning for close to 15 years. After 10 years at Schwab, he founded DeVoe & Company in late 2011 to help wealth management companies optimize their business decisions. The company has since supported well over 100 firms in valuation, consulting, and investment banking engagements.

While at Schwab, Dave served as managing director of Strategic Business Development, leading Schwab's Transition Planning platform. David also oversaw the Strategic Business Development sales team, serving large national clients, consolidators, independent broker-dealers, and turnkey asset management programs (TAMPs) and was director of Practice Management Programs, responsible for developing and managing a suite of programs to help advisors with business-critical issues, including transition planning, compliance, and human capital.

Rob Francais, CPA, CEO, Aspiriant

Rob is a cofounder and chief executive officer of Aspiriant. As Aspiriant's CEO, Rob spends most of his time driving the firm's vision and expanding its culture into new markets. Under Rob's leadership, Aspiriant has grown into one of the largest independently owned wealth management firms in the country.

Rob began his career in the personal financial and investment planning profession in 1988, and has launched several successful businesses and business lines within larger organizations. He was a cofounder and CEO of Quintile Wealth Management, which merged with Kochis Fitz to form Aspiriant in 2008. Prior to starting Quintile, Rob was a tax partner with Deloitte & Touche, LLP, in the Los Angeles office and head of its Technology Industry Practice for the Southwest Region. Over the years, Rob has been a regular guest lecturer on economics at UCLA and has taught taxation at the University of Southern California.

Charles Goldman, President, CEO, AssetMark

Charles Goldman is responsible for leading AssetMark, Inc., as president and CEO.

An industry veteran with deep experience working with independent advisors and broker-dealers, Charles was president of Custody & Clearing at Fidelity Investments and previously served in a number of senior roles at The Charles Schwab Corporation, culminating in his heading Schwab Institutional, the predecessor to Schwab Advisor Services. He has also served on boards of several companies, including Personal Capital, and industry organizations including the Foundation for Financial Planning and the Certified Financial Planner Board of Standards, the standards-setting body for the financial planning profession in the United States.

Mark Hurley, CEO, Fiduciary Network

Mark Hurley cofounded Fiduciary Network in 2006 and serves as its CEO. The Fiduciary Network team provides strategic consulting and long-term financing assistance for each of its partner firms, working closely with them to help engineer transitions of management and equity to produce durable business entities.

Prior to working at Fiduciary Network, Mark was chairman and CEO of Undiscovered Managers, LLC, a mutual fund company he founded in 1998 and sold to JPMorgan Chase in 2004. Before that, Mark had positions at Merrill Lynch and Co. and Goldman Sachs & Co. and served as a presidential appointee at a bureau of the U.S. Treasury Department from 1990 to 1992.

Eric Kittner, Principal, Moneta Group

Moneta Group principal Eric Kittner works with his clients to build solid financial plans through fully understanding his clients, educating clients about realistic goals, and preparing for potential curveballs.

Eric earned his BA in accounting from The Catholic University of America in Washington, D.C. He also attended the London School of Economics. Prior to joining Moneta, he worked at Arthur Andersen and then spent time as a tax associate at RubinBrown, LLP.

Looking to build relationships and have a more proactive role in his clients' lives, Eric joined Moneta as a professional consultant on the Sheehan Team in 2003. He was later promoted to principal.

Dustin Mangone, Director, PPCLOAN

Dustin Mangone serves as the director of the Investment Advisory Program for the acquisition financing needs of investment advisors nationwide. Dustin is a 2002 graduate of Texas A&M University with a background in marketing and finance and is a candidate for the CFP certification. He spent two years as a financial advisor providing retirement planning for nonprofit organizations before joining PPCLOAN in May 2005. With more than 10 years experience as a cash-flow lender, Dustin has underwritten more than $190 million in funded loans supporting hundreds of business owners across the country who are looking to grow their businesses through mergers, acquisitions, buy-ins, buy-outs, and succession plans.

John Henry McDonald, Founder, Austin Asset

In 1987, John Henry McDonald founded Austin Asset, and it became one of the first fee-only firms in Austin, Texas. During his 30-year career, McDonald was recognized for being an advocate and educator in the wealth management industry. He has been a crusader for transparency and disclosing hidden fees and commissions. His vision to "build the premier financial planning firm in Austin" culminated in the successful transition of leadership to coauthor Eric Hehman in 2007 and his ultimate retirement from the firm in 2014.

He continues to give back to the Austin community through his board service with Austin Community College, Austin Classical Guitar Society, and other philanthropic endeavors that reinforce his long-standing credo: "You can't outgive a giver."

Elizabeth Nesvold, Managing Partner, Silver Lane

Elizabeth Nesvold is managing partner at Silver Lane Advisors, a mergers-and-acquisitions advisory firm specializing in the asset and wealth management industries. She has advised on more than 150 M&A, valuation, and strategic advisory assignments in her 24-year career. A well-recognized expert commentator on the wealth management industry, Liz cofounded the first M&A advisory group for the sector in 1998. Her sell-side clients have included wealth advisors, trust companies, multifamily offices, institutional and alternative managers, investment counselors, financial planners, investment consultants, and financial technology firms.

Robert D. Oros, Executive Vice President, Fidelity Clearing & Custody

Bob Oros is executive vice president and head of the RIA segment for Fidelity Clearing & Custody, a unit of Fidelity Institutional. His team provides custody platform, brokerage services, trading capabilities, practice management, and consulting services to RIAs, including strategic acquirers, professional asset managers, and retirement recordkeepers.

Prior to joining Fidelity in 2012, Bob was executive vice president and national sales manager for Trust Company of America, responsible for sales strategy and relationship management. From 2008 to 2010, he held various positions with LPL Financial, including executive vice president and general manager for LPL Custom Clearing Services, president of LPL Insurance Associates, and executive vice president of acquisitions. From 1998 to 2007, he was with Charles Schwab, with positions in sales and product strategy.

Bob has a BS in business administration from Central Michigan University and has completed graduate work in finance at Walsh College.

Philip Palaveev, CEO, The Ensemble Practice

Philip Palaveev's firm, Ensemble, focuses on creating team-based, multiprofessional financial advisory businesses aimed toward sustained growth, profitability, and enhanced value. Ensemble also works with broker-dealers and custodians in creating practice management services for their advisors.

Prior to launching Ensemble, Philip served as president of Fusion Advisor Network, a network of independent advisors. From 2003 to 2008, Philip was a principal at Moss Adams LLP, an accounting and consulting firm with industry-leading expertise in practice management, where he led market research and consulted with hundreds of advisors and several top broker-dealers.

Rebecca Pomering, CEO, Moss Adams Wealth Advisors

Rebecca Pomering has been chief executive officer of Moss Adams Wealth Advisors, the wealth management division of Moss Adams, since 2008. Prior to that Rebecca spent 11 years as a management consultant with Moss Adams LLP, consulting to many of the most well-known wealth management firms in the country on business strategy and management. She is regarded as one of the leading experts on the business of wealth management and is a prominent speaker and writer.

Rebecca represents one of the very few examples of a consultant to the wealth management industry having moved into an executive role in management of such a business enterprise. She is able to put her wisdom in strategic planning, organization optimization, and mergers and acquisitions into practical application throughout Moss Adams Wealth Advisors' multioffice operation.

Bob Schiller, CPA, Cassady Schiller & Associates

Bob Schiller is a founding partner of Cassady Schiller & Associates, Inc., where he specializes in providing tax and consulting services to a wide range of privately held companies and their owners. In the past 25 years at Cassady Schiller, Bob has expanded his expertise to include taxation of high-net-worth individuals and gift, estate, and trust taxation. During that time, Bob has overseen a tremendous growth in the number of estate and trust clients served at Cassady Schiller.

Bob graduated from Xavier University, summa cum laude, with a BS in accounting. He also earned an MBA, with a concentration in taxation, from Xavier University. He is a certified public accountant with more than 30 years' experience, all in public accounting.

Joseph A. Sheehan, Principal, Moneta Group
Moneta Group principal Joe Sheehan serves his clients as their family CFO by incorporating Moneta's core values and serving as his clients' advocate in every situation.

Joe graduated from Vanderbilt University in 1974 with a BA in economics, and then spent seven years as a pilot in the U.S. Navy. After leaving the Navy, he earned his MBA in finance from Northeastern University, and then returned to St. Louis to work in his family's business. In 1991, Joe joined Moneta as a principal financial advisor, or family CFO. In addition to serving clients as a family CFO, Joe is the past CEO/COO of Moneta Group.

Joe and his wife, Caroline, have twin sons. Of all of his many accomplishments, Joe is most proud of his family.

Anne Shumadine, Chairman and Founder, Signature
Anne Shumadine is the chairman and a founder of Signature. In addition to leading the firm and working with the firm's clients, Anne is a leader in the Hampton Roads business community. Anne has been honored nationally and across Virginia as an outstanding legal professional and as an accomplished advisor to families of wealth. Anne has served on the boards of numerous nonprofit institutions, including the Board of Visitors of Eastern Virginia Medical School, Virginia Wesleyan College, the Chesapeake Bay Foundation, ACCESS College Foundation, ODU Educational Foundation, and the Wellesley College Business Leadership Council.

In 2011 Anne received the Citizen Lawyer Award from the William & Mary School of Law, the Barron F. Black Community Builder Award from the Hampton Roads Community Foundation, and the LEAD Hampton Roads' Visionary Award for business leaders.

Jeffrey Thomasson, CEO, Oxford Financial Group

Jeff Thomasson is the CEO and serves on the Board of Directors of Oxford Financial Group, Ltd., which he founded in Indianapolis in 1981. In addition to the leadership roles at his firm, Jeff continues to devote his professional expertise in serving individual families' financial and investment planning needs.

Oxford has grown to become one of the nation's leading independent, fee-only wealth management firms, handling more than $20 billion in assets for business owners, physicians, select institutions, and others of affluence throughout the Midwest and 37 states. Oxford has offices in five Midwestern states, 20 partners, and approximately 150 colleagues who work with clients in need of multigenerational estate planning or investment consulting. Oxford has consistently been named among the top five independent wealth management firms in the country.

Mark Tibergien, CEO, Pershing Advisor Solutions

Mark Tibergien is chief executive officer of Pershing Advisor Solutions, a BNY Mellon company. Pershing Advisor Solutions is one of the country's leading custodians for registered investment advisors and family offices. Mark has worked with public and private companies on matters related to business management, transition planning, and strategy formulation since 1976. This includes hundreds of independent registered investment advisors, broker-dealers, investment managers, insurance companies, and other financial services organizations in the United States, Australia, Europe, the Middle East, and Canada.

Prior to joining Pershing in 2007, Mark was partner-in-charge of the Business Consulting group, chairman of the Financial Services Industry group, and partner-in-charge of the Business Valuation group for Moss Adams LLP. Previously, he had been president of a bank and of a business training and consulting firm and a principal in an investment management and business valuation firm, following a career as a print and broadcast journalist.

Randy Webb, Jr., President, CEO, Signature

Randy Webb, Jr., is president and CEO of Signature, in charge of the firm's strategy and business development. Prior to joining Signature, Randy spent 18 years with Bank of America, where he was part of the bank's mid-cap investment banking group. He previously worked as senior vice president in the corporate finance group of Bank of America's predecessor institution, NationsBank. Randy is involved in the communities that Signature serves. He sits on the boards of the Virginia Museum of Fine Arts Foundation, the Portsmouth General Hospital Foundation, and the Elizabeth River Project; most recently headed strategic planning for the For Kids organization; serves as treasurer for the WHRO Board of Directors; and has been involved in the delivery of TEDXRVA during the past three years. Randy is a graduate of the business school of the College of William and Mary, and he earned his undergraduate degree from Hampden Sydney College.

Keith C. Wetmore, Chair Emeritus, Morrison & Foerster LLP
Keith C. Wetmore is the chair emeritus of Morrison & Foerster LLP, one of the 25 largest law firms in the United States.

From 2000 to 2012, he served as chief executive partner of the 1,000-lawyer global law firm. During his tenure, the firm more than doubled revenue to over a billion dollars annually and tripled net income, as well as expanding internationally and domestically in key financial and technology centers. Morrison & Foerster thrived under Keith's leadership, and remained committed to its legendary core values: superior client service, legal excellence, a culture of collegiality, a market-leading commitment to diversity, and its renowned tradition of pro bono excellence and community service.

In addition to his continuing roles at Morrison & Foerster, Keith serves on the Board of Directors of North Highland, a fast-growing information technology, marketing, and healthcare consulting firm.

About the Authors

Eric Hehman is chief executive officer of Austin Asset. Eric joined Austin Asset in 1997, became a principal in 1999, and CEO in 2007. In 2014, Eric completed the seven-year transition plan providing for the retirement of the firm's founder.

Under Eric's leadership, the firm has been awarded top national financial advisor honors in *Worth*, *Mutual Funds*, *Bloomberg's Wealth Manager*, and *Medical Economics*.

Beyond Austin Asset, Eric is a progressive influence for the next generation of financial planners and is a respected thought leader for best management practices throughout the industry. Sharing his story to encourage other next-generation leaders in their professional growth and managerial accomplishment fueled the fire that led to *Success and Succession*.

Eric is active in leadership of professional and philanthropic organizations, nationally and in the greater Austin area, including Regional Board President of the National Association of Personal Financial Advisors (NAPFA), founder of the Financial Planning Association (FPA) Austin Career Day, Capital IDEA, Central Texas Estate Planning Council, and the Make-A-Wish Foundation of Central and South Texas.

Eric is especially effective serving in leadership roles with early-stage organizations as they set out to achieve entirely new impacts within their communities. These have included Haleycurls for Hope, LifePastor, and Nineveh Ministries. In 2013, Eric was honored as the winner of the Austin Under Forty Award in the category of Finance, which recognizes a select group of young executives for their outstanding professional achievements and significant contributions to the community.

Eric is a graduate of the University of Texas at Austin with a degree in business economics. He earned the CFP® designation in November 1999, one of the youngest Certified Financial Planner professionals in the nation at that time.

Eric is a native of Austin, Texas, where he lives with his wife, JayLeen, and their four children: Christopher, Conner, James, and Jenna.

Jay Hummel is a senior vice president in the corporate strategy group of Envestnet. Jay is responsible for ensuring the company remains focused on building its technology and human capital around the business outcomes or opportunities advisors face on a daily basis. He spends much of his time consulting with the company's largest Registered Investment Advisor (RIA) clients and prospects, helping them build and deliver on their strategic vision through their partnership with Envestnet.

Prior to joining Envestnet, Jay was the president and COO of a large RIA based in Cincinnati, Ohio. His background is in public accounting and business consulting. In his five years at Deloitte, he helped manage the day-to-day operations of worldwide services to the Procter & Gamble Company, including the implementation of the Sarbanes-Oxley regulations and the early integration of the Gillette acquisition. Prior to joining Envestnet he also served as a manager and oversaw corporate planning for the Aon Hewitt Financial Consulting Company, Ward Group.

Jay has been active in leadership roles on both civic and business boards, including Audit Committee chair and board member of Alliance Business Lending, a regional asset-based lending company, and the Cincinnati USA Regional Chamber's Agenda 360 planning board. He served as president of Give Back Cincinnati. Jay is the cofounder of Fuel, an incubator focused on supplying start-up grants to emerging civic leaders. Jay is a frequent speaker at industry conferences. *Success and Succession* is his first book—but not his last.

At age 26, Jay was named to the Cincinnati Business Courier's "40 under 40" list, recognizing him as one of the Midwest region's top up-and-coming civic and business leaders. In 2014, he received the University of Cincinnati's Jeffrey Hurwitz Award, recognizing the university's top alumnus under the age of 35. He is a graduate of the Carl H. Linder Honors PLUS program, with undergraduate and graduate degrees in accounting from the University of Cincinnati. Jay resides in Cincinnati, Ohio, with his wife, Valerie, and their two sons, Cooper and Dylan.

Tim Kochis has over 40 years of experience in the personal financial and investment planning profession, serving clients and managing professional services firms since 1973, most recently at Aspiriant, before transitioning away from the CEO and then chairman role in 2012. He was a founder of Kochis Fitz, one of Aspiriant's predecessor firms. Prior to that, he was head of Personal Financial Planning for Deloitte & Touche and, before that, for Bank of America.

In 2010, the U.S. Financial Planning Association conferred on Tim the P. Kemp Fain Award for exceptional career-long contributions to the financial planning profession. In 2006, he was awarded the inaugural Charles R. Schwab Impact Award for leadership among independent advisory firms. The University of California Berkeley Business School Extension, where he cofounded one of the industry's first academic programs and taught evening classes for 18 years, created an annual award for teaching excellence in his name. As chair of the CFP Board's Board of Examiners in the late 1980s, Tim was responsible for supervising the creation of the first comprehensive examination now used throughout the profession to qualify CFP® candidates.

A member of the Estate Planning Hall of Fame, Barron's ranks him among the Top 100 Independent Advisors in the United States, and the *San Francisco Business Times* ranked him first among the top independent wealth managers. *Financial Planning* magazine has twice listed him as one of the profession's "Movers and Shakers" for many years of leadership in industry organizations such as the CFP Board of Standards and the

Foundation for Financial Planning, as well as for his founding role in the Financial Planning Standards Board (FPSB), the global certification authority for the financial planning profession, having served as its chair in 2005.

Tim's earlier books include *Wealth Management* (2nd ed., 2006) and *Managing Concentrated Stock Wealth* (2005), of which he is writing a second edition. He's currently at work on a book on wealth management for the Chinese market, with coauthor, Zhang Bei, PhD.

Tim serves on several nonprofit boards: the University of San Francisco, the Asian Art Museum, and The Asia Foundation. He also serves on the Charles Schwab Investment Management Co.'s ETF and Mutual Funds board.

Tim received his Bachelor of Arts degree from Marquette University, his JD degree from the University of Michigan, and his MBA from the University of Chicago. He was awarded a Purple Heart during his service in the U.S. Army in Vietnam.

Tim lives in San Francisco and Santa Barbara, California, with his wife, fellow writer and muse, Penelope Wong.

Index